Your Three Horses

Courtney,

Thank you For

everything

Contract

Thank you for
Everything

Your Three Horses

Desire, Passion & Persistence

Applying a New Life's Philosophy

Written by Todd Radus

www.ToddRadus.com

Cover Art & Design by

Cat Badger

www.cbscenic.com

Printed in the United States of America

"An amazing read. I recommend it highly"

Dr. Greg Reid
International bestseller Author.
www.GregReid.com

"Your Three Horses" is not another book about creating success by simply dreaming and hoping magic will occur. Rather, "Your Three Horses" offers a practical framework for achieving success. The author discovers this framework through the nitty-gritty of trial and error, determined faith and love, and trying again and again. This is not a necessarily easy path, but it's a path that any of us can courageously take."

Jason Freeman
Author of Awkwardly Awesome: Embracing My Imperfect Best
www.jasonwfreeman.com

"An amazing read! Todd gives you the benefits of his life-long wisdom! Read this book and implement its lessons....you won't be sorry!"

Todd Moser

Contents

Special Thanks

A huge thank you to my wife Catherine for her undying love, support, and guidance during our journey together; she's the focus of my energy -- the brightest light in my life. Also, thanks to John McMullen for his unwavering friendship and continued support. Additionally, thank you to Greg S. Reid for his inspiration. Last, but not least, is Larry Steinhouse; the man who encouraged and supported me in achieving all my dreams.

It wasn't until I had the support of these people that I truly believed in myself and had a solid trust in my own abilities to pursue my dreams. It wasn't until I found their combined guidance and support that I was able to bring all my dreams and goals to fruition. They are living proof that who you surround yourself with affects you the most.

Thank you all from the bottom of my heart, you have my eternal gratitude.

Foreward

As a personal development, financial, and real estate investing coach, I often have people come to me who truly want to better their life. Sometimes I make the mistake of prejudging them. In the case of Todd Radus I made that very mistake.

Todd came to me wanting to learn how to invest in real estate. He told me he was "in between jobs" and, "financially", things weren't all that great. Todd lived two hours from my office and I told him he would be more successful if we had face to face coaching meetings. I thought this distance would make it difficult for him. I listened as he tried to convince me to *let him hire me* as a coach. I continued to have concerns that Todd might be throwing away his money by not being truly committed. He persisted, and every time I threw an obstacle, or objection, as to why I didn't want to coach him, he came back with a sincere promise that he wouldn't let me down. I finally caved, took his credit card info, and started his coaching.

That night, I went home to my wife and told her the story of my newest student. I told her how I was afraid I just took this man's money and I didn't think he would benefit from me or my coaching.

BOY, WAS I EVER WRONG!

Todd came to his first appointment driving a beat up 2002 VW Beatle with 180,000 miles on it. I wondered if he would actually make it home after the meeting. In this meeting, Todd told me his desire of being successful.

Like me, he was a big fan of Napoleon Hill and the laws of success and attraction. We talked about his dream to be a personal development coach and a writer. My immediate reaction was to tell him to do it! I believe I said something like, "Get off your ass and get started!" He told me about a book concept he was writing, and I said, "Go for it"! He objected, stating he was afraid no one would like it. My response was, "So what? Make it a goal to get it published". He said he was going to finish it and promised it would be a good one!

In one appointment, Todd told me he wanted a black Cadillac and, sure enough, he showed up with that very car at a later appointment. Then he said he was going to buy his first rental property, and within weeks of joining our school and coaching program, he did it!

A few weeks ago, Todd told me he finished his book and gave me a PDF copy of it. He asked me to read it and then graced me with the opportunity to write this foreword. I have to say, I did it again, I prejudged, or at least thought, "What if this book is terrible? What would I tell Todd, and how do I write a forward for it?"

I am here writing this forward because this book is fantastic! Todd nails the path to success. His "Your Three Horses" analogies to describe Passion, Desire, and Perseverance are spot on!

The funny part is that I have been procrastinating in writing this forward and reading the book gave me the encouragement and passion to write it.

What I thought might be a burden has become an honor that I am not even sure I deserve. This book is going to change the life of anyone who reads it!

Yep, I'm the coach he refers to in a chapter of this book, and, at this point, the student is clearly becoming the master!

Enjoy this book as I have, and remember, you can do anything with God at your side and your Three Horses at your disposal!

Larry Steinhouse
Author, Speaker,
Personal Development Coach,
and Founder of
InvestorSchooling.com

Introduction

Let me start off by introducing myself. My name is Todd Radus. I never considered myself to be better than others and I still don't. On the contrary, I saw myself simply as a dreamer who worked hard to accomplish his goals.

This book is the culmination of my life's experiences along with the results I've had from studying and applying Napoleon Hill and Dale Carnegie's philosophies on success, combined with works of Wallace D. Wattles.

It wasn't until I discovered Napoleon Hill's philosophy that I began to realize that I already had many of the keys to success. However, I was still missing a few of the most important details in actually achieving a life of success.

In this book I want to bring to you my Three Horse Philosophy so that you may experience the success and happiness I have found in my life. In my experience, this philosophy makes success much easier than it is made out to be. The Three Horse Philosophy is a summary and guide to understanding the philosophies of success; it is the culmination of a lifetime of experiences that has made me who I am today.

The ideas of these men lead me to a revolution in thought on what it means to become successful; they gave birth to the Self Improvement movement that has helped tens of thousands of people find more success and happiness in their lives. This philosophy based both in personal growth and how to deal with others, if followed, has only one logical conclusion: that **you will demand of the universe whatever it is you want, and you will earn the right to possess it. You**

will be a better person, a happier person and a more successful person.

Like many young people, my own arrogance and pompous nature prevented me from understanding and attaining success. It wasn't until I reached a point in my life that I asked myself the most important question; I would come to realize the importance of asking this question.

The exact day or time isn't entirely clear, but there was one simple question I asked myself, *"How could I have achieved some of the amazing things I achieved and still not be successful?"* My definition of success was to have enough money to enjoy all the freedoms life has to offer while ensuring my wife would never need for anything and could pursue her dreams.

At the time, I was 47 years old. While I never truly worried about money or allowed those kinds of stresses to stop me from doing anything, the desire to provide for my wife and allow her to live her dreams were driving my own thoughts and desires.

There was something missing in my life, keys to success that I was not yet in possession of. I had done everything that was expected of me -- I worked hard, drove myself and achieved goals other people only dreamed of.

My bank account, however, did not show the results of my efforts. It turned out that there was a major flaw in my thinking; I thought money was earned by working for a wage. It was this thought, and the belief that earning money can lead to success, which was truly holding me back from what I viewed as success. This realization was one of the keys to changing my mindset to that of success. I now understand that earning money for a wage is different than making money. I also learned that each person has their own perspective and what one person views as success is not necessarily what another person views as success.

When you earn money, you can go to work and earn an hourly or salary wage. You can also earn money by contracting your skills out to others. When you make money, you do not do the labor; rather, you are paid for providing something. To be successful financially, what you provide needs to become self-sufficient and not require your time and efforts to maintain it. While there will be costs, such as maintenance and occasionally some time involved, for the most part, you are creating money.

The perfect example of this is owning an apartment complex. You have dozens of people paying you for their homes. You pay others to maintain those homes, collect the rents and process the paperwork. The apartment complex is self-sufficient. You have set up a system and that system operates on its own. You have done the hard work of which you were not initially paid for doing. In the end, your apartment complex generates a stream of money that is indefinite. *This* is making money, rather than earning it for a wage.

You went the extra mile by doing the work, putting up the capital and organizing the business, all of which you were not paid to do. You were working for the future (Increased Returns) and doing it for free. The business now pays you dividends. If your mindset is one of *"I need paid now or I'm not doing it"* you will never be able to achieve true financial freedom. Investments of all types require work and effort for which you are not being paid. In many cases they require you to put money up or borrow money in order to get started.

There are many other investments you can get into. Paper investments, such as stocks are one. In all cases however, the goal is to have that investment pay you long term.

Success is individual, of course and you may not see my version of success as your own. I am sharing my experience. I no longer wanted to put all my time and effort into making others wealthy while I struggled and had no time to spend with my family.

In order to do this, to find my version of success, I would have to find new ways of making money while using the skills I was best at. I would have to increase the mental image of what it was I wanted. I would have to find my dreams and set new, much higher, goals. I would have to shoot for the stars and do it without worrying about how much I was getting paid.

In the following chapters we will discuss what it takes to succeed. Most importantly, I will address where and how I was wrong throughout my life on the quest for success. This is my own perspective, inspired and cultivated by the ideas of others, through the books I have read and the mentors I have followed.

While there were many other teachers and many books that I've read, these two books, *"Think and Grow Rich"* and *"How to Win Friends and Influence People"* had the most profound effects in my life.[1] The philosophies taught in these two books on success are very similar in nature and work in a complementary manner.

This book might serve as your introductions to these philosophies, however, never stop learning or seeking new perspectives because with each view you study, there is much

[1]See "Further Reading Recommendations" chapter for more information on these books.

to be learned. Each view will have its own gold buried inside; your perspective is your own, and you will find things in the teachings that others may not. To some, it may involve reading hundreds of books, from the esoteric to business practices, in the attempt to bring it all together to use in your own life.

Never be discouraged because the universe is wiser than you -- it's always guiding you. Once you find your niche and apply the philosophies to your goals **nothing will stop you**. I say this book is an introduction because there is no way I could possibly put down in words the entire scope of these philosophies in this one book. You will have to seek out more about these philosophies from a variety of perspectives.

My hope however, is that this book will inspire you to take what I teach here, to go further with it and embrace these philosophies to better all aspects of your own life. This philosophy can help you find success, wealth and happiness. Your own perspective on what it means to be wealthy, successful and happy will be the driving force behind what it is you accomplish.

While many people seek financial wealth, others seek spiritual fulfillment; others may simply want to find a partner to go through life with. Whatever the case, you can use these philosophies to set your goals, figure out what actions you need to take and find what it is you are seeking.

Napoleon Hill laid out the groundwork for personal improvement and success, continually stressing their importance. Dale Carnegie focused on these topics with razor precision on personal growth and interacting with others. Interestingly, both authors were on separate paths yet discovering complementary philosophies. Their books came out only a few years apart. I find it interesting that the universe had put two of the greatest self-improvement minds on separate paths with harmonious works.

I had achieved great things but I never had the final combination that would allow all these things to grow into greater success. The Three Horse Philosophy covers the basics of how we line ourselves up for success by using our minds to create our reality and using actions to find and create opportunity in our lives. There are rules in addition to the Three Horse Philosophy that we will cover in detail. These are the laws of the universe and how to apply them to everything in it.

There is the Law of Attraction, which is commonly misunderstood. It is not my belief that simply meditating on what you want will deliver it to you. I will cover how I practice the use of the Law of Attraction in the most practical way I can. Then there is the Law of Increasing or Increased Returns. The application of this law of nature can be seen everywhere around you and applies to you as well. We will also cover the Law of Economics and how no one, or any organization or concept, is above it.

We will discuss your balance sheet and how it affects the outcomes of your efforts. The entire Three Horse Philosophy is structured so you will understand the power of your mind and how to apply that power to your life. Every aspect of your purpose and goals in life is wrapped into the chariot, yourself and the horses (the power of your mind).

No matter what it is you want from life, you can have it. When I speak of success in this book, I'm speaking of what it is you see success as being. If you apply these rules with the Three Horse Philosophy and combine that with the study of the complete philosophies, I have no doubt that you will find all the success you desire. You will become a better person and you will surround yourself with quality people.

As you will see as you read this book, I had achieved amazing results with only small portions of the philosophy in action. You will also see that I suffered staggering defeats and setbacks. Some of these setbacks and outright failures took years to overcome. The small portions of the philosophy I was practicing, even if unaware of them, were continually delivering me to where I wanted to go.

Let's get started. I hope with all my heart that I can help you achieve what it is you want to achieve, that when reading this book you will take from it some valuable lesson that will better your life. If I have done that for you, then I will consider this book a complete success.

The Story of My Wife

A SMALL PORTION OF THE PHILOSOPHY IN ACTION

This is a heartwarming section for me to write. I get tears in my eyes thinking about her and what we have gone through. This story is also vitally important to success because it proves the points that I will repeatedly make in this book.

By examining both my story and her story, I began to form the Three Horse Philosophy. All of this happened before I had the inspiration for it. Much of it took place when we only had small portions of the philosophy in practice. Together, we achieved more than most would have ever expected.

Today, my wife owns a successful business. Of course, many people have achieved what she's achieved. However, we will start, first, by telling you that around 5% of people who graduate with a degree in the art field find success in the industry. Would you go to school for such a degree? Most of us would never consider spending nearly $120,000 at the turn of the millennia on an education with a less than 5% success rate. My wife is an artist. She went to an exclusive college for women to learn how to expand her natural skills and talents in doing artwork. Her talents were astronomical, as were the talents of her fellow students.

Why did she become a success while others ended up spending decades repaying loans and earning minimal salaries? Why would she find success when others couldn't? Did I play a role in that success? If so, how? These were all questions that needed to be answered. Careful examination of these questions was necessary to understand her success.

The story of my wife is the story of a young woman with dreams of becoming a professional artist. These dreams went all the way back to her childhood; a little girl who loved art simply for the sake of it. She appreciated even the worst pieces of artwork for what they were.

My wife grasped on to her talents like a person who had fallen off a ship with only a life preserver and the faith to survive. The most amazing part of her journey is that she did this without consideration of the risks. She stayed on her path without fear of failure. To her, monetary gain wasn't necessarily a measure of success.

The odds of her success were overwhelmingly stacked against her. Since I was 18 years older than my wife, I had more life experience that would provide guidance for her. However, she wound up helping me in ways I never could have imagined. The universe has a funny way of aligning things.

The odds we faced both as a couple and as business people seemed stacked against us. One thing we realized together is that if you base your success solely on monetary gain, you may find it hard to have any monetary gain.

If I was going to help her become the artist that she desired, I needed to stay out of her way. If I stepped in with too much force, it could cause resentment. Therefore, I had to watch her make mistakes, including the figurative burning her fingers and bumping her head, all the same mistakes and learning curves I had gone through. After all, mistakes are some of the best teaching tools in life.

When she was in school, I was working as a valet manager at a parking garage, making a decent salary that would help lessen the burden of her future financial debts, which in the end would benefit both of us. We spent tens of thousands of dollars on art supplies and other necessities for her schooling.

The valet manager job paid for the home, food, cars, clothing, and so on. Everything outside of class costs, which many of her fellow students were racking up into their future debt in the form of student loans, was being paid for at that moment. When it was time to buy a new tool for a project, we bought the best supplies.

If she needed it now, she would also need it in the future. See, there was no doubt that she would become a successful artist. All of our actions revolved around that belief. Sometimes we had debates about the costs of these tools but we would eventually decide to get the best supplies we could. To this day, many of those high-quality tools are still in her professional tool chest.

There was one issue we confronted together: Whether or not the school was preparing her for success in the real world. This is a relevant concern for most universities, and perhaps the entire education system as a whole. Colleges can be rather inefficient at teaching someone how to be successful.

This experience made me realize that most schools only teach people the basic, general knowledge of whatever the chosen field is. The philosophies of success are not being taught at most schools. There seems to be a belief that these philosophies are unneeded in the modern world.

I learned things about the art education world that made my skin crawl. One of the most damaging ideas instilled into her during this process was the crazy notion that if she did commercial work, she would somehow be some kind of 'sell out'. **Really?**

The thought of being a sellout - after amassing $100,000 or more in student loans while trying to make it in the corporate world - seemed insane. How were these young people going to make money in the art industry if the school was teaching them that by doing so they were selling out? Don't take things wrong, it wasn't as if the school had made this a normal part of their curriculum.

In response, we decided to sign up for any business classes and/or marketing classes that were offered; anything practical to assist her after graduation. **There were none.** She did, however, sign up for a two-hour seminar held by a successful graduate regarding the art business world. **That was it. That was all that was available to her for business education.** She learned specific and general knowledge about *making* art, but there were zero classes on how to actually apply those newly-found skills. Thankfully, the school now offers outsourced classes on business.

My wife worked hard during college. She even graduated second in her class, even though at the time she didn't know what her path would be, or what her goal was in becoming an artist. Her desires were fueled by her passion and carried forward with a persistence that is rarely seen in the world.

The negative influence of the art community's beliefs on selling out was so bad that when she was offered a job for $14.00 an hour working for a scenic art company, **she actually considered not taking it**. She believed it was selling out, just as she had been taught by her peers in school. After all, it wasn't in her field of fine art.

Funny thing, being an artist. For some reason, if an artist takes their skills to a trade and goes to work in order to make money, they are selling out on their own ethics, even though there are over a hundred thousand dollars in debt, with bills to be paid. The art student is then expected to live in a studio apartment while starving, making art until they die. After death, they might finally reach success.

After a discussion taking place over a period of time, she took the job. She based the decision to take the job on the fact that her student loans would be coming due soon. We also affirmed that she was fortunate to find any work in the art field in the first place. She realized that she would never know where this job would lead her.

Opportunities like this rarely come. I was relieved with her decision to take the job. She possessed something that others didn't -- she went the extra mile constantly; it was in her nature. I knew, in my heart, that the extra efforts she consistently put forth would bear fruit in the future.

Although the job provided a decent income, she wasn't happy with the company's management. However, one thing college taught her was the value of persistence, a lesson not taught in many schools. It also provided the initial professional networking that helped lead her into her future career.

The obstacles and setbacks never stopped her as she determinedly followed her path. She moved over those obstacles as if they were not even there, having a singular focus. Her desire and blind obsession to become an artist allowed her to do all the hard work that was needed. She put in endless hours, never stopping.

There were many times she needed to be convinced to take a break; sometimes she would be in her studio at the school until classes started the next morning. She carried this drive and dedication into her career, spending endless hours in her personal studio and on projects.

She gained skills from this first job that eventually lead to her landing a position in the movie industry working as a scenic artist (and making very good money at that). This new career in the scenic art industry would start to get her close to twice what I was making a year, but this isn't where her true success flourished.

The true success was in the fact that she had been building her own scenic art company for nearly a decade now. As this is written, she's on a project for a major corporation in Texas. She will net more than an entire year of my last job's salary. She hires other artists and pays a very good hourly wage, twice what the company she originally started with offered her.

She pays more than other companies because of her willingness to go the extra mile to acquire compensation for everyone that travels with her. She understands that traveling is difficult and because of her kind heart she ensures that everyone is fairly compensated.

In her resolve to treat those who work for her fairly, she makes sure they are fairly compensated for having to work away from home. She's rewarded for her generosity by getting some of the best people to work for her. She always goes the extra mile for her employees. In turn, they do the same for her.

As of today, this now grown and experienced woman is in full command of her future. She makes enough to pay her debts off. She is successful and in high demand by those in charge of scenic art in the movie industry. Although she isn't making millions yet, she doesn't gauge her success purely on monetary gain. She loves what she's doing and thrives on the challenges that present themselves.

She has done something that 95% of other artists never do: turned her art degree into a successful career. Using her raw talents, persistence and drive, combined with her education, she made the necessary adjustments to take advantage of the opportunities that were presented to her.

> *It's her drive, determination, and desire that made her successful.*

In this case, the student became the teacher. I knew how to run a business. After all, I only helped her start her business and take it to corporate status. She needed to learn everything there was to learn about running a business on her own. She did the hard work, only occasionally receiving my help. If I did everything for her, she wouldn't have gained the experience necessary to succeed. How could I have mentored her in such a way that she became successful, when I couldn't even do it myself? **These would become profound questions that needed to be answered if I was ever going to be successful at the level I wanted to be successful at.**

I had the general and specific knowledge necessary, and even some of the keys, but **I wasn't reaching my goals**. For the first time, I finally asked the question that would lead me down the path of my own success:

> *"Why am I not successful?"*

It was this business side of the relationship with my life's partner that would give me one of the major keys to finding my own success. The key was to ask her to help me with the self-evaluation questions that would need answered; I had to find the answers to fully find the meanings behind the questions.

It may be obvious to you what was missing, but I wasn't seeing it. I was blinded by my own arrogance in the matter. This was where I was deriving this deep belief that I could do anything. I definitely didn't think I needed help doing it. This was a major flaw in my thinking.

I believed that I knew better than everyone. Even those who were doing exactly what I wanted to do but couldn't. Once I did some self-evaluation, it became painfully obvious that I had been foolish and stubborn.

My wife, on the other hand, had an obsessive desire to be an artist. She had a passion rarely seen and she had the persistence to never stop, no matter what setback she was facing. She had the wisdom to listen to mentors and employ people who could help her do the things she didn't know how to do. She listened to the advice given by other professionals.

None of this was coincidence. She was literally born to be a successful artist. The universe had lined things up for her; it had put me in her path, not the other way around. I had the knowledge she would need to become a successful artist, a desire she had been feeding her entire life. I was a gift to her, not because I'm something special or some sort of visually-perfect person but because I had knowledge she would need.

It was my experience that she would draw upon. In turn, she became the greatest gift for me. Her relentlessness drove us down the path to success. My knowledge guided that path. Whether she intended to or not, she would teach me through example what it was I was missing, and she would become the teacher. We would work as a team. We would feed off each other and become successful together. We had a perfect relationship; working in harmony to reach a singular goal. This goal was our success, both as a couple and as professionals.

Another blatantly obvious connection is our dedication to one another, our willingness to give to each other without reservation. There is nothing I would not do for her and there is nothing she hasn't done for me.

Our love creates the physical energy used to transmute desires into reality. This is called the sexual energy… the energy of the physical body transmuted into a powerful force in organizing your desires and amplifying their effects on the physical world around you. As long as you don't abuse it or spend your time seeking physical gratification.

One final note for the women who read this book (of course, it may also apply to men): My experience with my wife during her time in college was my first true exposure to radical feminism. During her time in school, it was hammered into her head to look for misogynistic men. She was told they were out to hold her back, keep her down and own her. This distrust from others came to the surface during some of her first encounters with men in business when she was starting her business.

Yes, there are sexist men and there are sexist women. That's a fact that isn't going to change and you are not going to change it, so don't waste effort trying. This is a perfect example of a society-based obstacle.

There was a deeply ingrained fear in her subconscious that surfaced upon her first professional encounter with a man who didn't respect her. His lack of respect was going to affect the outcome of her work unless she handled the problem. She had no real idea whether this was because she was an artist or a woman running a new business. She just didn't know what the cause of the problem was.

Years of negative nonsense had polluted her mind. I reminded her of what she had done so far, where she was going, and that **she was in charge**. I told her that, sure, he might be a sexist. Or, he might just be a jerk. In either case, she was going to have to earn his respect with her actions in order to complete her job -- whether she wanted to or not.

She would have to master her own thoughts and mind in order to get past this obstacle. She did it, though. Although she was convinced he didn't like her, she worked with him nonetheless. Who cares why he didn't like her? It didn't matter. You are going to run into people like this. The reasons for their lack of respect, hate, or anything else, are unimportant.

Never allow someone's negativity to affect you.

In any case this man didn't respect her, so she was going to have to earn his respect through her actions. I say *"who cares"* for a reason. It's likely you will never know the real reason for someone's lack of respect for you. They may plain-and-simply not like you, and even that's okay.

Not everyone is going to like you. It's your choice how you respond to this, both internally and externally. The reasons are unimportant. It's up to you to not spit out any internal belief of your own when dealing with people like this. You shouldn't try to change what people think about you. If you simply move forward without attaching any negative emotions to these situations, you will be able to resolve them. In all situations like this, negativity is unwanted. You want to remain positive and never embrace another person's bias, no matter how it makes you feel. Try not to empower them by embracing their negativity.

Some people are just negative in nature. If you start making excuses for your inability to deal with someone and taking the easy path out, saying something like, *"Well he's/she's a sexist... I can't do anything with them,"* you will likely fail. A failure or major setback is exactly what's going to end up happening if you allow others to impose their ignorance on you.

What you are doing in your own mind is empowering that person as a racist, sexist or misogynist. Even if they don't actually fit any of these labels, they will in your mind. What's in your mind is what matters most. You relinquish your own power and abilities to this internal belief which may or may not even be true. Even if it is true, you still need to get past it. It was negative views and embracing of excuses like this that caused my wife to feel powerless.

Those who tell you the simple truth: that your failures are your own fault, are frowned upon, called cruel and heartless. In actuality, it is those who are embracing your excuses that are actually encouraging your failure. With all good intentions aside, those who coddle your emotions and embrace your excuses are aiding you in your failures.

Blaming others for your failure is an excuse. No one causes you to fail except you. Most disturbingly, today's society generally seems to accept excuses for failure. There are scores of people who will embrace your excuses.

Furthermore, anything you desire to overcome can be overcome. Anything that you believe will hold you back **will absolutely hold you back**. It's up to you whether to give your belief credence or to simply move past it. Too many times people use excuses to write off their failures rather than taking the time to evaluate them and learn from them.

My wife could very easily have taken the easy path to defeat and allowed this man to ruin her project or her reputation. However, this didn't happen because she chose not to let it happen. She didn't embrace the excuse and take the easy way out. She faced the issue and found a resolution to the problem. No matter what he did, he actually had no choice in the matter since it was up to her whether she would succeed.

While she did seek counsel and support, she wasn't looking for someone to coddle her feelings. She was looking for someone to assist her in resolving the issue; I provided that support. She knows that I don't believe in the idea of allowing someone else to affect me or cause me to fail. She was simply looking for help to clear the hurdle in order to move past the issue with her fellow contractor. When you seek support in this manner, don't go to those who will coddle you. Go to those who will tell you the truth because they will be truly helpful.

The story of my wife is one of success. By seeing how she converted a childhood dream into a successful career by harnessing desire, persistence, and blind obsession, we can all learn valuable lessons. She didn't know how success was going to happen but was certain it would happen. When obstacles were laid before her and she suffered setbacks, she struggled through and never gave up.

The Three Horses

DESIRE, PASSION AND PERSISTENCE

The Three Horses Philosophy will not be easy to master. While it may seem straightforward, mastering it will take effort, time, and dedication. In order to master the philosophy, you will need to use and incorporate it into your life. The beauty of it is that your mindset will have to change to one of success. **Your Horses are the power of your mind itself**. Your mind creates the thoughts which manifest your greatest desires. The manifestation of your desires isn't magic in any way. There are things we must do to bring our desires into reality.

The basic version of the philosophy will allow you to master it. If you harness the power of Your Three Horses, they will lead you to success.

The Three Horses are as follows:

- **Desire**

- **Passion**

- **Persistence**

When you hold the reins of trust and faith, you will guide the power of the Three Horses to your favor. You will be able to ride your chariot of purpose to any goal you can conceive. **You will be able to achieve anything you want, provided you believe you can.**

Imagine yourself standing on your chariot of purpose, or the major purpose of your life. By doing this, you already possess your chariot. When envisioning your horses, you must stand upon the chariot which is constructed of your purpose and goals. The reigns you hold on to are faith and trust. You must hold these reins tightly because trust and faith guide Your Three Horses toward success. Your desire becomes obsessive, your passions harnessed and completely focused. Your persistence is the driving force ensuring that you never stop moving forward.

Creating this affirmation in your mind is hard to master but is the key in reaching your goals. By envisioning these things as physical objects, you can use this imagery to stay focused on your intents. The chariot is your ultimate goal. The first power guiding your chariot is your obsessive **Desire**. The second is your unwavering **Passion**. Your third is unending **Perseverance**. Failure is not an option; it's a choice you should never embrace.

There is a price for driving the chariot and **giving yourself is the greatest payment**; it's the people we help along the way that provide the positive energy needed to fuel the entirety of the journey. This means going the extra mile and doing more than what is expected, which also means that you should be doing more than what you are being paid. We should try to bring others along with us on our journey by helping them achieve their goals. There is no greater reward than helping others -- this alone can provide the fuel needed to power your chariot.

The Three Horse Philosophy is a basic guide to success. When all aspects of this philosophy come together and work in harmony, there is nothing that can stop you from achieving your goals. You can realize your purpose and can harness the powers of your mind to guide your desires and passions while reinforcing them with persistence.

Each time you better yourself, you increase your own power. When you harness the power of all Three Horses they will work together and nothing will stop you. They will carry you through the harshest conditions and the darkest of nights, never wavering and never giving up.

Each action that you take is within your control. After all, the imagery of the horses and the belief in yourself is created in your mind and **the mind is where your true power lies.** By having faith and trusting in this process, you will be able to guide the unlimited powers of your mind to achieve greatness or find success and happiness.

You will draw in like-minded individuals who can assist you. The more you perfect yourself, the more you will draw both people and things to you that will help you achieve your goals.

While this is the basic philosophy, the act of achieving it can be a challenge, but a challenge we need to be willing to accept. The metaphoric imagery is only a tool to help you remember what you need to do to succeed. The real power lies within your mind and if you can harness that, you can change your life immediately.

The Rider

YOU

The rider is you. Your will must be strong in order to achieve your goals since it will require much effort from you. Weak-natured people are incapable of riding the chariot or controlling their horses. If you are weak-natured, the remedy is to immediately **start strengthening yourself**. It's a choice, to grow the strength needed to reach your ultimate goals or destiny.

This simply means you will need to build the mental fortitude to manage your thoughts because they are the powers behind finding success. There are no skills that can't be learned or practiced once you decide to take up the challenge. Once a person has the internal fortitude to admit their weaknesses, work to resolve them, and grow from their failures, they will have the strength and resolve to master this philosophy.

When we grow from our setbacks and failures, we increase our strengths which allow us to master our weaknesses. Being able to evaluate, self-evaluate and make proper changes are the keys to long-term success.

The rider must be mindful of themselves, especially their thoughts and beliefs. The horses do not respond to negativity, selfishness or greed. A rider must be charitable and good-natured to harness the power of their horses, one who shares their journey and assists others, tames their mind and takes control of their life.

Your strength comes directly from your mind. The rider needs the fortitude to steer their own life in the right directions while allowing them to lead. These three powers: Desire, Passion and Persistence are the basis by which you choose to succeed or fail.

To allow you to see the power within yourself, I would like to tell you a story from my life. These events laid the foundation from which I would build my future successes upon. The story involves one of my greatest achievements and shaped how I approached goal achievement and what I believe is possible. When reviewing these experiences, I came up with the rider portion of my philosophy, because the rider is ultimately who's in control of your life.

The story starts when I was just sixteen and still in high school. I had a few jobs at this point in my life, mostly in fast food. After a very short stint of drying cars in the Michigan winter at a local car wash, I responded to an ad for a salesman at a local department store.

After all, freezing in subzero temperatures for 4 hours a day after school to dry cars in a car wash at minimum wage didn't seem to align with my life's goals. I'd be surprised if it did for anyone. The cars would come off the wash and I would become soaked while drying them. The dryers blew hot air that swirled around the bay and kept the area fairly warm. That was until the main door was opened to allow the car to leave and cold air would rush in. When that door opened, I would feel every damp spot on my clothes from the cold Michigan winter air and become chilled to the bone.

Fortunately, I got the interview for the sales job. When I went there I was convinced I would get this job. After all, I really needed it. Arriving for the interview, I saw that the store was extremely small, even by the standards of the 80s.

The store was cozy, pleasant, and everyone who worked there was welcoming towards me; the environment made you want to come back. Even at my young age, I recognized the brilliance behind this.

I went into the interview. The manager was sitting behind a desk with piles of papers and various other office items strewn about. After being asked all the typical questions, I informed the owner that I would do whatever it took to ensure I became a great salesman for him. I was totally serious since I needed out of the car wash job sooner than later. I remember thinking about how nice it was to walk through the doors and leave the Michigan winter behind me as the warm air flowed past me when entering. A few days later, he called and asked me to come in again.

I was extremely excited, I wanted this job and I wanted to do something different. The car wash was miserable and cold. I went to the second interview convinced I had the job as a salesman.

It was snowing that day. As the wind was whipping the snow around the back parking lot, it chilled me to the bone. The owner was sitting behind his desk, still a mess, and smiled at me. He welcomed me in, shook my hand and had me sit down. He started to explain the situation to me.

Since I was underage, the owner felt that a sales position wouldn't be a good fit for me. I jumped in softly, interrupting his sentence. I was clearly disappointed about not getting the sales job. I asked if there were any other positions available. I explained I would take whatever position he had. In hindsight, I realize it was obvious that I was desperate for a new job.

After being informed that this was the reason he called me in, he offered me a position as a stock boy. I took the position and ended up stocking shelves and working the sales floor, occasionally tagging along with one of the appliance salesmen. The salesman was a great guy, a wisp of a man who was clean cut, dressed nicely and always smelled of fine cologne.

It was this salesman who taught me the value of appearances. He taught me that even though we shouldn't judge someone by their looks, it was important to look good. No matter what you believe, your appearance does have a lasting effect on people. This is most important when you first meet someone, as there is only one chance to make a first impression. It would be more imperative in my role as a salesman since I would be interacting with a variety of customers.

He also taught me a lesson which has proven true to this day: Don't judge a customer by their appearance. Many people may be in jeans and a T-shirt but you never know what they can afford until you ask. The full lesson was simple: look good for those who are judgmental and never judge someone on their appearance.

I took this advice further and applied it to my life in other ways -- I did this because of his teachings in appearance. That choice would later pay off as I pursued my career in business management. He was right in that we are judged upon our appearance.

The salesman explained that the reason for not hiring me as a salesman was that older adults do not readily accept teenagers as sales representatives. He further explained that in order to be a successful salesman you should be able to relate to the customer since they are actually buying more than the product.

However, I still wanted to be a salesman. They made more money and commanded a little more respect than a stock boy.

Both the owner and sales associates were impressed with my people skills, which took me by surprise since I didn't have many friends in high school. I wasn't a loner or outcast, but rather someone who didn't get into the same things my fellow classmates had interest in.

One day, my boss came up to me to see if I would attend a sales seminar with him and the salesman that was training me. The seminar was the following weekend and was not a job requirement. Although a voluntary, I eagerly accepted the invitation.

I was not familiar with the philosophies of success back then, so this seminar would be my initial exposure to them. The keynote speaker that day was Zig Ziglar. While I don't remember much from that seminar, I clearly remember being mesmerized by Mr. Ziglar.

There were some things he taught that have stuck with me to this day. I don't remember exactly how the message was stated but Zig Ziglar was a fantastic speaker with a remarkable wit. He told us that no one can tell you what's possible for *you*, that only you can decide that. What I learned that weekend would come to play a large role in my life. It was similar to what my fellow coworker spoke of when training me, *"Don't be discouraged; if you know you can become a salesman then it will happen."*

Even though I wasn't a salesman yet, my boss seemed to like me and constantly encouraged my learning. The conference and speech that Zig Ziglar gave would have a far more profound effect on me then I originally realized. There was something else he said that stuck with me, even though at the time it didn't seem very sales related.

One quote by Ziglar that deeply resonated with me was, *"It's your attitude, not your aptitude that determines your altitude."* Even being a young, hot tempered man, I would remember to keep that attitude in check as best as I could. Even in the face of extreme adversity, I would always do my best to stay positive. Since I was trying to achieve something that was just out of reach, these two ideas seemed very applicable at the time. Don't let anyone tell you what you can or can't do and it's your attitude that determines the outcome.

The store manager eventually made me a jewelry salesman. I don't think it was because he wanted to, but rather that the salesman who worked that counter took ill and had to leave his job. When asked, I jumped on the opportunity immediately. I learned early in life that the ability to recognize an opportunity and take advantage of it was a skill needed if you ever wanted to advance in life.

Over the next year, I made very good money considering I was just a teenager in high school. This time was great for me as I polished a lot of my people skills while selling jewelry. Jewelry is something I rarely wear myself, of course, but this did not mean I couldn't sell it.

Eventually my time as an aspiring salesman was drawing to a conclusion. I had learned a lot during those couple of years.

The next story is the story of my first triumph. It's also when I started to use a philosophy that I was barely aware existed.

I had a love of airplanes, and had built many models; I dreamed of working on and flying them. I ended up deciding to be an electrician – more specifically, an electrical tech working on aircraft. To do this, there were two options: one was to go college; the other was to join the military.

Student loans were out of the question. After all, my father was a teacher and didn't have the extra money to send me to school. After looking at the numbers, I realized that taking out student loans would mean a lifetime of debt. That simply was not acceptable, so it was off to the military.

After scoring well on the ASFAB tests, I decided to try getting into the Air Force. Sadly, they didn't have any open positions in the field I wanted. Remember, this was during the mid-80's; there was no war so finding open positions in technical fields wasn't easy. Apparently, I wasn't the only one with the idea of going in the military for technical training.

Next up was the Marines. They explained that the Marine Air Wing was small and only an elite group of men could be in Marine Air Wing. They recommended the Navy. In reality, I was avoiding the Navy at all costs. I didn't want to go out to sea and had no love of ships. The idea of living on a ship wasn't very appealing to me.

The recruiter for the Navy was happy to see me. At the time I figured it was because he was lonely. Isn't the Navy everyone's last choice of service? It was definitely mine at the time. I told him I wanted to work in aviation as an electrician. After going over my scores, he told me that I was well qualified. However, he couldn't get me into the Aviation Electrician School for a least a year.

That simply wouldn't work; I needed to get started sooner rather than later. Being young at the time, a year seemed like an eternity and I hadn't mastered patience yet. I was ambitious and wanted to get out of my father's house, to be on my own more than anything.

I went into the recruiter's office and asked to enter immediately and be a part of the school as soon as it was available. Well, this was a mistake because he was a lonely man and needed recruits. He said that I could still request to enter the school after I was at my assignment. He also explained he could get me the aviation rating, which would put me into a squadron or into aviation support.

This would have to do, so I signed up and several months later I was off to boot camp. There is nothing like going through boot camp during a cold winter at the Great Lakes Naval Training Center near Chicago Illinois, otherwise known as Great Lakes Boot camp or "Great Mistakes." It was cold and miserable there, only adding to the stress of being in boot camp. However, we did a great job and graduated with honors as the top unit. We received the honor of wearing the white leggings and carrying a mass of flags boasting our accomplishments. When the ratings and orders were handed out, I was graciously given the coveted green stripes of an aviation mate.

My orders were to meet up with VA-35, an attack squadron out of Naval Air Station Oceana in Virginia. I had a week at home with my family and then was off to join my squadron. Once there and settled in, I immediately went to the career counselor.

Strangely, there was no real career counselor, just a chief who was assigned those duties, having various other duties also. I went in and asked about becoming an Aviation Electrician. He informed me that I could request the school, but it was more likely I would get approved after re-enlisting.

This was a disappointment like I had never experienced in my life. After all, I had just signed away 4 years of my life for this. The preconceived image in my mind was not that of being a grunt worker in the military for the next 4 years. Nor was it to be doing the jobs that anyone with a designated job rating didn't want. I was nauseous, and needless to say, very angry about the whole thing.

The recruiter didn't lie; he simply wasn't very upfront about my odds of getting approved for school. I went back and stewed in some self-pity for a few days, barely speaking to anyone. When asked what was wrong I just shrugged and would say, *"It's nothing, I'm fine."* In my mind, I wasn't.

In spite of my distress, it was time to put my anger aside and start thinking clearly. There was no time for self-pity or wallowing in defeat. There was no way I was going to waste the next 4 years doing something I didn't want to do. I checked my attitude, gathered my thoughts and started organizing a plan. I had no idea how I was going to make this happen, I just knew it was going to happen. First, I would have to find out how I could get my rating without going to the school or waiting to re-enlist to become what I wanted to become.

I went back to the chief and asked him if there was any other way I could become an Aviation Electrician.

"There is, but I've never seen anyone do it."

"What do I have to do?" I responded.

"I have never seen anyone achieve a technical rating without having gone to school or without being assigned to that department. I have seen people achieve lesser ratings but if you can pass the test, you can get your rating."

Aha! There was a light now, an opportunity; something Zig Ziglar spoke a lot about. Something I knew could be seized when recognized. This would later be related in my philosophy through the concept of desire and purpose.

"What Test?" I asked.

The Chief seemed a little annoyed at this point as he shuffled some papers around, almost as if he was looking for something. He looked at me and said

> *"Pass the test, it's the same test the A school students have to pass to receive their ratings, but again, I have never known anyone to achieve a technical rating like electrician without the school or being assigned to the shop."*

> I smiled at him and asked, *"Can you get me all the books to study for the test?"*

> *"I can,"* replied the chief.

> *"Please order me the books…I'm going to pass that test."*

> *"Okay,"* he said, *"now get out of here, I'm busy. I'll call you when the books come in."*

Several weeks went by while I worked my tail off washing airplanes, humping chains around the flight deck, and doing oil servicing on the jet engines while learning the sign language to talk to pilots and all the other aspects of how to be an effective plane captain. Plane Captains take care of the aircraft when they are on the ground, helping service them and ensuring everyone's safety during flight operations; they help the pilots get the planes started and ready for flight.

Since I had to do this, I was going to go the extra mile and do it the best I could. See, sometimes you will be pushed around until you achieve the status of your assignment…in this case; it was becoming a plane captain.

Plane Captains are lovingly called "roof rats." While the title seems lofty, their job is to do all the stuff no one else wants to do: washing planes, topping off oil, carrying the tie-down chains, securing the planes to the deck of the ship, and so on.

One day a call came into the shop; it was the Chief was requesting I come to his office. I knew what it was about and went to the office. I was excited -- there was a light at the end of the tunnel. I knocked on the door and he called me in. He looked up at me and pointed to a stack of light blue colored manuals.

"There you go son. Those are all the course books for Aviation Electrician. Good luck."

I smiled while picking up the ominous stack of books. I had already studied some government issued classroom books while in boot camp and knew that this was going to be a challenge.

After arriving back at the shop, everyone was curious as to what the books were. Most of them just looked at me like I was nuts or had three heads and a tail after hearing the story. This was not encouraging to say the least.

One man was especially rude about it calling me an idiot for thinking I could do this. One of my fellow "Line Rats" approached me and in a sincere manner asked,

"Do you think you can do this?"

I smiled at him and said, *"I don't think I can, I know I can, after all, don't let anyone tell you what you can or can't do."*

Over the next nine months, I worked 10 hours a day, 5 days a week while on land. When we were out at sea, the shifts were 7 days a week, 12-hours a day. Being the newcomer on board, I had the night shift. Every spare moment ashore and off duty was spent studying. When not studying, I was in the electrical shop driving everyone crazy with questions.

Most people didn't see or respect the effort, but I didn't care. Many people were constantly telling me that I was going to fail miserably. In retrospect, these people were more comfortable criticizing than supporting; after all, it's easier to do. It allows them to justify their own circumstances and failures. These are the kind of negative people I learned to ignore early in life, another aspect of the philosophy that I would come to understand.

I realize now that I had picked up more than I thought from my exposure to Ziglar's lecture. I had been exposed by my sales job and the sales conference to the philosophy that provides the keys to success. The few crumbs I picked up had changed me in ways I didn't realize.

After my third pass through the books it was finally time to take the test, and I knew I was ready. There were several people who seemed as if they didn't want me to pass, mainly the ones who thought I was crazy for trying. However, many wished me luck and I went to take the test.

It was a long and tedious test filled with the typical government style questions. I wasn't sure how I did once I completed it. Feelings told me that I had passed, but with all the negativity seeping into my thoughts from those around me, I had doubts. It would be weeks before the results came back. I went back to work praying that I did well enough to pass. I felt like I had when I was working at the carwash, dying to get the job as a salesman. I wanted desperately to move up and be something different.

Eventually a call came into the shop. The chief had my results! When I walked into his office, the skipper and the chief were there waiting. The chief immediately stood up with a smile on his face. The skipper walked up to me and stuck his hand out; I shook his hand as he smiled at me.

"Congratulations son, you're an Aviation Electrician, and I must admit, none of us thought you were going to pull this off. Good job."

The Chief reached over and shook my hand. *"Didn't think it could be done but you proved me wrong kid, nice work."*

I was beaming; I couldn't believe what just happened. The Chief explained that the skipper would present my aviation wings officially at the next squadron meeting. When the next meeting came, the squadron Master Chief told me to stand beside him in the front row.

Several months later, an opening was available in the electrician shop and I officially became an Aviation Electrician, and eventually went on to work final check on the flight deck. This entire event was a lesson that has stuck with me to the present day. Don't let others tell you what's possible and don't give up trying. It was my persistence that allowed me to become an aviation electrician.

When my wife made me a shadow box for my military accolades, I had those wings displayed in the box. This was the biggest accomplishment I achieved while in the service. The wings sit directly below my squadron patch. While others may look at the box and see medals from the Gulf War and the ribbon bar, my eyes always go to those wings. They are proof that if you learn the rules you can shape the game of life in your favor.

I learned it was true that no one can tell you that you can't do something. The experience also taught me that **Desire**, **Passion** and **Persistence** were traits worth holding on to.

It's our desire that guides us in reaching our goals and it's our passions that fuel our drive to achieve our goals. Our persistence carries us forward, never allowing us to give up or believe anyone who tells us we can't achieve something. You are in control of your life; you are the reason for both success and failure. Choose to succeed and never accept failure.

The Chariot

PURPOSE

The chariot is your purpose in life; it's the foundation on which we built our success. It's what you stand upon as the Three Horses carry you on towards reaching your dreams and goals. If you don't know your major purpose, then choosing a major goal is a good place to start. I didn't know my major purpose when I started so I chose a major goal. In striving for that goal, I found my purpose in life.

Your major purpose or major goal reaches far beyond a simple goal. A major purpose is different from a simple goal because you are reaching for the stars. I have a saying I like to use: *"Reach for the stars and you may reach the moon or Mars, reach for the ceiling and you never leave the room."*

You will have many goals during your journey through life, but your major purpose is the end destination. Your major purpose must be written down; it must also contain the three components that make it greater than just a goal. Write down your major purpose, what you will pay for it, and a timeline in which you expect to achieve it.

Again, if you don't know your major purpose, choose a major goal and apply the same philosophy. Your purpose will eventually come to you. The need for major purpose and definitiveness of action cannot be understated. Napoleon Hill once said it perfectly:

[2]"**Napoleon Hill, Think & Grow Rich (New York NY: Fall River Press, 1937).**"

"Whatever the mind can conceive and believe it can achieve."[2]

We should take a few moments to understand this concept thoroughly. You cannot achieve anything if you have no goals or purpose in mind. Many people wish or dream of having things or some form of success. Without writing it down, focusing on it and striving for it, nothing will come of those simple wishes or dreams.

While it may seem nonsensical, it isn't. What your mind envisions it sends to the universe and, in turn, the universe sends it back, not distinguishing between good or bad. This is the basic Law of Attraction. This is why your goals and purpose must be constructed of positive imagery in your mind. What I mean by this is: you need to be positive and know you will reach your goals.

This concept is very well proven and can be seen in nearly every inspirational story of success. It's proven by the book in your hands because I believed it would be written. Almost nothing that surrounds us came into being without someone imagining it first. In the story of my wife and in my story we can see how we both believed in what we were doing and we both were able to achieve those goals.

Everything that has ever come to be was first conceived in someone's mind. In a moment of imagination, somebody conceived of every device, tool, and modern comfort and item we use to make our lives easier.

It's said that necessity is the mother of invention. If that's the case, then imagination is its father. After all, imagination is required to think up and develop the idea for the item which will satisfy the need.

No achievement is ever reached without it first being conceptualized in one's mind. This is why your purpose in this philosophy is your chariot and becomes the foundation upon which you build your success and find happiness. You can go nowhere, nor can you ever move forward, without having definitiveness of purpose. You must know what you want, that you're going to achieve it, what price you're going to pay for it, and the timeline in which you expect to achieve it. In order to achieve your major purpose or goals start by doing the following:

- **Write down your major purpose.**

- **Write down what you expect to pay in order to achieve your major purpose.**

- **Lastly, write down a timeframe in which you expect to achieve your major purpose.**

The major purpose is the foundation of achievement in that it provides the necessary goals you are striving to reach. This should be well thought out with deep consideration to your ability to reach the goal and a realistic path in which you can achieve it. Play to your strengths here; focus on what you're good at or willing to become good at. Do this within both your mental and physical capabilities, be realistic. Unrealistic goals are wishes not based in reality; therefore they are not true goals or purposes.

When you first start, write down what it is you want to achieve. For some people this will take some time to think about and reflect on. For others, they already know what those goals are.

Exclaiming that you want a million dollars, or even $100 million, is not a major purpose; it's a wish and wishes have no foundation to strive for, they are simply fantasies and dreams. Proclaiming you will have a million dollars doesn't manifest a million dollars. Proclaiming that you will have a million dollars by providing the needed widgets to the masses is putting a path to the million dollars in front of your desire to have the million dollars. This gives the universe a way to provide the opportunities to reach the goal of having the million dollars.

For instance, Thomas Edison wanted to create an incandescent light bulb. He wrote down what he wanted to accomplish, and then began moving towards that goal. After around 10,000 attempts, he finally achieved that goal and created the incandescent light bulb. While this would make him rich, his main goal wasn't to be rich; it was to provide light without the need for a candle. This new light would be for the betterment of all mankind.

Now, there is a purpose! His price was the labor it would take to achieve the goal, which was over 10,000 attempts to create the bulb. He was not deterred by his failed attempts and used persistence to keep moving forward towards his goals. Each failure was a learning experience and was written down in his notebooks. He learned in the process how not to make a light bulb in order to find out how to make a light bulb.

The reward was riches for Edison and light for all of humanity. Your goal and purpose does not need to be so grandiose, but they do need to be definite. As I was striving to be an aviation electrician, my goal was definite. My wife's goal to be an artist was definite and she never questioned it; it was just going to happen.

The timeline establishes a point in which you expect the universe to have delivered the opportunities to achieve your goal, this too must be realistic. When I started to study my books to become an aviation electrician, I wanted to have it done within the year. Thankfully, it was done in only 9 months. At the time I didn't know about the format for forming a purpose and achieving it, I just stumbled onto it accidentally. Even though I hadn't written it down, I focused on it regularly, during nearly every waking minute my mind wasn't occupied by other thoughts or the tasks at hand.

The forming of a purpose and goal is necessary to achieving anything you want to achieve. If you don't have a goal then you can never reach it. As mentioned, wishes are not goals. Desires backed by passion support goals but do not create them. Your mind must be used in order to create the goals you want to achieve. It's your thoughts, imagination and mindset that matter when developing your major goals or purpose in life. No one can do this for you, you must do this yourself.

Every goal I ever achieved in my life was simply because the goal was targeted and the steps to achieving it were laid out in my mind. This was providing focus followed by taking the actions needed to achieve it.

Shortly after my discharge from the Navy, I ended up homeless in Florida. This, of course, was not my goal but would teach me another lesson. The experience would stick with me and the fact that it was a lesson would be verified later through my studies of this and other philosophies of success. The lesson is that many failures are caused by a bad choice of partners; **having the wrong associations can, and usually does, lead to failure.**

The story goes like this: When I was in high school, I loved art class and was pretty decent at it. Recognizing that most artists never make a living doing it, I never pursued it. You can see the difference in mindset between my wife's desire to be an artist and my lack of desire.

After getting the typical Navy tattoo on my forearm, I thought about doing tattoos. So, I bought some equipment and learned how to do them. I did quite a few while I was in the service and became pretty good at it. Here again we see not just wishing or dreaming of doing it but putting a plan into action to actually do it.

When I was close to getting out of the Navy, a personal friend (who had saved some serious money while in the service) brought up the idea of opening a tattoo studio. Wanting to go into business for myself, I found the idea intriguing. He proposed an even split in owning a tattoo studio together. He would run the business end and finance the studio, while I would do the artwork and train new artists.

This seemed more than fair since I had been through a divorce and was paying child support at the time, and I hadn't saved any money. I only had a few thousand dollars to my name and no plan for what I was going to do upon my discharge from the Navy. I was about to learn the difference between a dreamer and a goal-driven person, as well as the difference between a dream or wish and actual goals.

After shaking hands and agreeing to go into business, he gave me an address where he would be staying a few months later when he was discharged. Upon my discharge, I went back to my father's house in Michigan to wait for the opportunity to meet my new partner in Florida. There was only snail mail at the time, no e-mail or cell phones were available. There was no instant communication, as there is today; everything took time and required a level of faith in someone's word that isn't generally needed today since we can communicate instantly.

Later on, I received a letter confirming our plans and a date to meet him. I wrote back confirming my intentions to be there. When the time came, I packed up my belongings, put them into the car and headed to Florida.

I remember arriving in Florida and driving towards the ocean. As I passed the swamp, the stench was somewhat overwhelming. It's hard to describe if you have never experienced the smell of a swamp -- it's a cross between sewage, rotten fish and stagnant water. It was the middle of summer and the swampy smell hung in the air like a blanket. This would eventually smell like home to me, but for now it took some getting used to.

I arrived at the address ready to get out of the car and see my friend. I made the turn onto a dirt road that wasn't well maintained into a trailer park. To my dismay, the address was assigned to a run-down, dirty trailer with no cars out front. I pulled in and looked around, getting a little nervous about the situation I was now finding myself in. This was no upscale trailer park by any standard. It was, frankly, the epitome of the stereotypical trailer park. I was expecting aliens or a tornado to greet me, but no such luck.

I walked up to the door, all the while inside my mind hoping I had the wrong address. I knocked and heard a lot of shuffling around inside before a man who needed some serious hygiene lessons answered the door smelling of body odor and alcohol.

"Have you seen my friend?" I asked.

"No, I haven't heard from him since he was deployed to the gulf," said the man.

Nervous, I responded, *"Did he write to you and tell you to expect me?"*

He just shook his head no and looked at me blankly. I explained the situation and he simply had no idea about it. This put me in a pretty grim situation. It was obvious that my so-called friend hadn't told this man about our plans. I decided I would get a room and wait a few days in hopes of hearing from him through this man I had just met. Remember, I'm waiting for a letter to arrive informing me of the situation. My friend was supposed to have been there a couple of days earlier, but it wasn't unusual for the military to cause delays, so I decided to be patient. Setting aside the money necessary for incoming bills, I found a room and settled in.

It wasn't long before my money was running short and my friend hadn't arrived yet or contacted the man at the trailer. My position was starting to look pretty dismal. I had applied for a few jobs, but without an address, there was no luck in finding one. It would seem people didn't want to hire drifters. I imagine there are many people who drift through a state like Florida, so I could understand the concerns of employers when it came to having an address.

I went back to the filthy trailer several more times looking for my friend who never showed up, called, or wrote. I was on my own and needed to find a way to make it. I needed to either change my goal of having a tattoo studio or seriously revise my plan. I was being presented with a serious setback, though at the time I viewed this as a challenge.

I decided I was going to stick to the plan to own a tattoo studio. I struck a deal to split whatever I made doing tattoos with the guy in the trailer for a place to stay until I had enough money to get my own place. He would bring me the work and I would split the money with him. This sounded like the perfect Plan B, though I almost immediately regretted my decision after he showed me to the spare room.

The carpet was so filthy it seemed to have a coating of grease on it. He pointed to a stained mattress on the floor, apologized for the condition of the room, and told me I could stay there. At this point, I was in a desperate place and thanked him for the room. While I wasn't happy about the situation, I was grateful that he took me in.

I immediately swelled up inside, ready to pack it up and call my father for money to get home. However, he wasn't very supportive of the idea in the first place and asking for money to come home would have been unacceptable. I was at a critical point; I could choose to give up and fail or move on and develop a plan to achieve my goals.

I decided to move forward and try to complete what I came to Florida to do. I was going to own a tattoo studio. I bought a mattress cover and thankfully had a military blanket in the car. It would be the first and last night I slept in the house.

That evening, several people came over for tattoos. Amazingly, my new friend actually had held up his word. I was not comfortable tattooing there, but I had to do something. We did everything we could to sanitize the area. We split the money at the end of the night and I pocketed about $150.00. Not a bad take for my first night.

Feeling a little better about everything and exhausted from a night of hard work, I laid down to sleep. I felt much better about my position as I fell asleep. Several hours later, I was awoken by something crawling on me. Now, Florida is notorious for bugs and I knew this. While I was growing up, my family and I had been camping in Florida several times.

On this particular morning, I reached up and flipped the light on to see roaches on the walls, on the bed, and all over the floor. They scurried around running from the light. This was a new experience for me; in my mind it was completely unacceptable and horrific. With my socks sticking to the carpet, I got dressed, grabbed my stuff, and left.

I decided to spend the next month sleeping in my car at night. Desperation forced me to shower and clean my clothes at a local YMCA and laundry mat. I returned the day after and told the man that I had met a girl and that I was going to stay with her. I had never actually met a girl. I was making an excuse so I wouldn't have to stay with him any longer and also so I wouldn't hurt his feelings or ruin our arrangement.

I still wanted to do the tattoos, so we made new arrangements for me to stop by and do the work at certain times. He delivered more business than I ever expected. He had a steady line of people who wanted tattoos.

I was saving every penny so I could get my own place. Eventually, the insurance and registration on the car expired after I neglected to pay the bill. I still drove around looking for places to live, and one day I came across another trailer park. This one, however, was nice and well kept.

At the trailer park, there were people walking around and there were a lot of military base stickers on the cars. This made me feel very comfortable since I was familiar with military people and felt welcome around them. I put it in my mind I was going to stay here and put my mind to work again, just as I had done before. I didn't realize it at the time, but I was putting together little nuggets of a philosophy I had yet to fully realize. Desire and persistence were about to go to work for me again.

After going in and explaining my situation to the manager, she informed me that I would need $1200.00 down.

Additionally, I would have to get the power and phone turned on by myself.

I only had about $600.00 at this point. I had to spend money as it came just so I could buy basics necessities. Every couple of days I was getting a room so I could get a good night's sleep and a long private shower. I went back several weeks in a row trying to find out if a trailer opened up and finally, one did.

I had saved up to about $900.00 at this point and told her I could give her $800.00 of it to hold the trailer. Graciously, she let me move in for only $850.00. Specifically, this was $425.00 for first month's rent and a security deposit of $425.00.

She took me to the trailer and showed me around. It was even furnished. She left the furniture because she thought it would be necessary if I were to rent the trailer. I now had a bed, dining room table, couch, and a small desk in one of the bedrooms. The power was even still on in the parks name. She said she would have the shut-off date set two weeks from then. I was extremely grateful for her kindness and consideration. I told her if she ever needed anything just ask. I told her that I was very handy and would be more than willing to help out if she needed it. Eventually she took me up on that offer. It felt so very good to give back when she needed the help.

I got back to work immediately since I still had the goal of owning a tattoo studio. My previous experience had taught me that I could do it if I put the work into it. I subsequently went around to every bar, to the beach, and to whomever I could find to tell them what I was doing.

Without realizing it, I was setting up and focusing on minor goals that would help me reach my major goals. When contemplating this philosophy, I realized that I had put wheels on my chariot. I had developed minor goals in order to reach my larger goals. We will cover this more in the chapter on The Wheels, or your minor goals.

It was only a couple of weeks before I was spending more of my time tattooing and was able to get up some real money. I upgraded my equipment to some of the best you could buy at the time. Meanwhile, I was putting money aside as fast as I could.

I was going to own a tattoo studio and nothing was going to stop me. I now had a singular focus, a definiteness of purpose. Nine months later, I opened a tattoo studio. After 3 months in the new studio, I realized that it would end up making over $300,000 that year. Unfortunately, this would all come crashing down shortly thereafter. We will discuss this a bit later.

The point of this is that without realizing it, I had set up a major goal and created a purpose for myself. I had developed time lines in my mind in which I expected to achieve these goals. I had harnessed my horses using all my desire, passion and persistence to achieve minor goals that would lead to my major goal. I had held on with faith and trust in both myself and in reaching my goals.

I had, for the second time in my life, developed a major goal and achieved it. I know that if you put these same principles to work for you, you can do the same. It all begins with having a goal to achieve -- in other words, having your chariot. Without it, there is nowhere to go to or any means of getting there.

Desire

THE FIRST HORSE IS DESIRE (OBSESSION)

Desire is the driving force behind your purpose. She is obsession when used properly. When you focus your desires on your major goals or purpose, it creates the mindset that allows you to pursue those goals. Without the goals, there is no chariot to ride on and no place to drive to and therefore, no reason for desire. Without desire there is no determination to reach your goals. Desire must be attached to the goals and carefully bridled with trust and faith in order to harness its power.

If desire becomes an obsession in the rider's mind then success is inevitable. When we obsess over our desires we create the drive and direction needed to reach our goals. When desire goes to work with passion and persistence, there is only one outcome possible: Success. Desire helps contain and guide the other horses while carrying the rider towards their ultimate goals. Your obsessive thoughts are manifested in reality since they are constantly in your mind, and these manifestations come to us in the appearance of opportunities.

You are constantly creating the mental imagery necessary to transmute the desire you have into reality. Desire is the means by which you give direction to and can turn the powers of your thoughts into reality. When you envision the desire in front of you, it becomes the mental projection of your wants and desires.

The Desire Horse symbolizes your goals and the projection of your purpose. Desire tells the universe what it is you want through the constant mental images created by you. Desire harnesses the Law of Attraction by which opportunities will be presented. It's through desire that we create our realities by projecting our subconscious thoughts.

Desire's action upon the universe comes from your internal subconscious imagery and belief in the results. The same principle applies to all living beings. We can validate her through some simple observations:

One example is that of attracting money. For instance, take the image of loose change and hold it in your mind. At the same time, envision your bank account growing from all these coins. Now keep your eyes peeled. You will start finding coins. Embed this into your mind subconsciously and you will find coins constantly. While those coins may well have been there already, your subconscious is now trained to find them and the universe will start to point them out to you. By the same principle, this is also how you learn to spot opportunities.

If it's not working, then you don't believe that it works. If you dismiss it as chance, it won't stop occurring, you just won't see it. We should be grateful for all the gifts given to us by the universe. Always send back gratitude for what you have been given. If you are not gracious for the gifts that you receive, you weaken Desire's ability to tap into the Law of Attraction.

To give you another example, I've convinced myself that I will receive signed books when I order them used online. Therefore, I have received signed books when I ordered them online. In fact, I've received 4 signed books in the last 3 months and all have been by some of my favorite authors. "**I will receive signed books**." This is the thought I embedded into my mind and subconscious.

A friend of mine from the past used to worry constantly that he would hit a deer on the road. He hit at least one every year, damaging his car and costing him money. He was constantly reaffirming his belief that he would hit deer while driving at night. In his mind, he saw deer on the road and the universe saw that it happened.

On the other hand, I have done just as much driving on those roads and when I think of a deer, I have pictured a deer staring at me on the side of the road. There are routinely a lot of deer and they are always on the side of the road. To date, I have yet to hit a deer. I would much rather find pennies using my thoughts than hitting deer while driving. **What is it you think about that comes to pass?**

Back when I was in my 20s, there was a medical emergency and I had to take someone to the hospital. During the ride, I constantly said the lights are green and pictured green lights over and over in my mind. I had traveled this stretch of road hundreds of times and had never made all the lights.

This particular day, every light was green. The universe helped me arrive as quickly as possible to the hospital. Instead of thinking the lights are red, or that I'm going to catch all the red lights, I was thinking the lights were green and they were. This had never happened before and I can't remember ever making that string of lights again after.

Obviously, there are some cases in which the universe can't give you what you want at that precise moment. If, however, you pay attention to what you're thinking, it starts to become apparent how much effect your thoughts do have on your reality.

In the book *The Self-Aware Universe*, Dr. Amit Goswami theorizes that consciousness came before matter. Accordingly, it was consciousness that created all matter around us. He believes that consciousness came first and created the material reality we see. His theory does lend credence to the Infinite Intelligence at work in the universe, as explained and taught by so many success coaches and self-improvement teachers.

This idea has also been described by Napoleon Hill and various other philosophers. While originally dismissed by most of mainstream science, this consciousness theory has gained more ground in the last few years. Various scientific observations have illustrated that consciousness affects reality.

One notable study is known as the "double-slit" experiment. The idea behind this experiment is to show that light is traveling as a wave until observed or measured, and then it becomes a particle. When it's in wave form it will show an interference pattern, but when in particle form it will not show the interference pattern.

When doing the experiment, photons of light are projected at two slits to see if the interference pattern emerges or not. This pattern shows the path of the light wave. If observed, the wave turns to a particle and no interference pattern emerges.

When the light is sent through the two slits and there is still a wave present, it will produce an interference pattern. However, when trying to determine which slit the photon goes through, things get interesting. When observed with cameras and detectors, the interference pattern doesn't show up at all, even if they try setting up detectors *behind* the slits. No matter what scientists do, if they try to observe the photons, the interference pattern fails to emerge. In other words, **mere observation affects the reality of the photons or light waves**.

Another group of scientists have tried a variation on the double-slit experiment, called the "delayed-choice" experiment. The scientists placed a special crystal at each slit. The crystal would split any incoming photons into a pair of identical photons.

With this setup, it was possible that physicists could successfully find a way to observe the logic defying behavior of photons. One photon from this pair should have gone on to create the standard interference pattern, while the other travels to a detector.

But it still doesn't work. And here's the really interesting part: it simply doesn't work when we attempt to observe. Even if the second photon is detected after the first photon hits the screen, it still ruins the interference pattern. This means that **observing photons changes reality**. It also changes events that have already happened.

This also seems to validate the idea that at the quantum level of reality, time seems to have no influence on quantum materials. After all, the events observed in this experiment show that changes are being made in the past.

If so, *what is stopping events at the quantum level from changing at any time in the past?* I believe this is applicable to thought, since thought is taking place on the quantum level. After all, thought are comprised of energy, and therefore, thoughts are a quantum interaction with the universe.

What I'm getting at is this: when you focus your thoughts (which take place at the quantum level) on a goal or material thing, these things are being lined up through all of time to come to you now (because of an interlinking of quantum materials, thoughts and material reality).

In Wallace D. Wattles book *The Science of Getting Rich*, he discusses how the Thinking Stuff of the universe materializes into what it is you desire. I refer to this as the "ether" -- just as Nicola Tesla did; it's all the same stuff! It would seem that Quantum Scientists are starting to validate these long-held beliefs. It would seem that the observations of philosophers might well be quantifiable through the logic-defying rules of quantum physics.

The most profound aspect of this is that there is no limit as to what could be created through thought. Granted, we cannot materialize a car that we want in our driveway, but we can materialize every event that takes place to bring us the opportunity to own that car, including the actual making of that car in the past so that we can have it now.

I realize that to those who are new to this, the entire idea may seem impossible. Yet, it would seem through observation we can validate these ideas. Additionally, we can now see through modern science that there is a lot more going on at the quantum level then we once thought.

Another experiment that is profound, yet rarely discussed, is that of the "quantum entanglement" experiment. If a particle is split into two parts, they always react to one another. If the rotation of one is changed, the other changes instantly. No matter how far apart they are, they change together to match each other's rotation. This shows us that on the quantum level, where your own consciousness exists, time and space do not inhibit your ability to project your thoughts.

Think about this for a moment: if you consider that everything started at a singular point (IE the Big Bang

Theory), everything is in one way or another interconnected at a quantum level. This could mean that your thoughts could be perceived not only on the other side of the galaxy, instantly, but clear across the entire universe.

Since thoughts take place at the quantum level, not the physical level, they become our direct line of communication with the entire universe. The universe responds to your thoughts. When you project the image of your desires, they are recognized by the universe. This is the reason desire is so powerful. The more you believe it will happen, and the more you focus on it, the more opportunities you will have to receive your desires. These opportunities are the means by which we can obtain our desires.

Scientists looking for answers that refuse to see the effects of consciousness remain baffled. Others are starting to see the light, so to speak. The reason scientists refuse to look at consciousness as a cause of the effects, and rather an effect of physical being, is simple. They believe that consciousness is an epiphenomenon of the brain. As a result, they don't even believe consciousness is real, because they believe it's an illusion created by the complexity of the brain. If it isn't real, in their minds, it can't have an effect on reality.

The danger in this should also be recognized. If you send out thoughts of fear or negativity, that is what ends up being delivered to you. The great prophets, theologians, and philosophers understood this.

The transmutation of thought into reality does, in fact, occur. While we do not yet know all the mechanisms, we do not need know them in order to understand the effects. We can recognize from both testimony and observation that when we focus on our desires, opportunities to achieve these desires start to present themselves. Regardless, we need to both recognize them and act upon them if we ever wish to achieve our goals.

Have faith in your desires. The universe reacts to everything you think, making your thoughts real things. It will then manifest in your reality in the form of opportunities, obvious while others are less so. This isn't to say, as mentioned, that if you picture a car in your driveway it will immediately appear. **That isn't how it works**.

What this means is that your desires are manifested by the universe presenting you with opportunities of all kinds. These opportunities will, in turn, lead to that car being in your driveway. In fact, you will more than likely be the one to drive it there and park it in place.

In fact, this was exactly how I received my car. I wanted one badly but had a limited budget, so I put pictures of used models up on my wish board and started shopping every morning until I found not only the car I wanted, but a great deal that I could afford.

While the car wasn't delivered to my driveway, the opportunity to own it was delivered to me. I needed only take the final actions to receive it. As I drove my old car to the dealer the AC started burning up, only further validating the need for a new car. As it turned out, I got a car for nearly the same payments of a previous car that I recently paid off. I sold the two cars, the one I had paid off and the one that smoked on the way to the dealership, making up the difference in cost. In the end, I bought the car I wanted with no effect on my budget.

By taking the actions needed and projecting my desires, the universe delivered me the opportunity to own the car I wanted at what I considered to be affordable.

Desire is the key to finding the opportunities which will present themselves and allow you to have what it is you desire. Knowing that you will reach your goals, coupled with the continual imagery of your goals in your mind, leads to reaching your goals –provided, of course, that you act upon the opportunities that are presented. When all aspects of your three horses (Desire, Passion and Persistence) are working in harmony with the rider and his chariot of purpose, success is inevitable.

Passion

THE SECOND HORSE IS PASSION (HARNESSED)

Passion is the second horse. Passion is the power of your focused emotions. Your emotions must be in the center of your mind, surrounded by guidance and control in order to harness and contain their powers. If your passions are left to run freely, they can become a destructive force. Much like a child who cannot control their emotions, passion must be held in check to master the philosophy.

Your passions must be in the middle, thus we describe it as the Second Horse. While passion is the true source of some of your greatest strengths, it must be controlled and managed. The power it brings to you is so great that it cannot be left to its own.

Passion is a wonderful thing when used properly. Examples include love, sexual energy, cheerfulness, and all other positive emotions. Passion can also be dangerous. After all, passion can be used in both negative and positive ways. To realize your dreams and hold on to them, your passions must be harnessed and their positive nature exemplified. The power of your passions is so great that it is capable of either uplifting you or destroying you.

Love is the most powerful force in our lives. This force is followed by the emotions of sex, happiness, optimism, empathy, and so on. Positive emotions, when harnessed and put to work in a positive manner, can fuel the entire chariot and all its components. Without passion, the chariot has little power. It is your positive emotions that allow you to focus on the goals at hand in a constructive way.

No matter whether you are working on a goal or seeking to live out your dreams, you must have some form of passion to reach those goals. I have heard people say that you should make your money first before trying to live out your passions. However, you must have a passion for making money if you ever want to make any.

When asked what my passions are, they are simple: my wife, and helping others. This is why I became a trainer, coach and philosopher. I study human nature combined with the laws of nature in hopes of creating a better world for all those I encounter.

In my own life, I had many uncontained passions. They ran wild and drug me down, feeding my anger and disdain. Most unfortunately, they too often distracted me from my goals. Even though my emotions were out of control for most of my life, they were still the fuel behind much of what I achieved in my life. Emotions were the propellant that sent me into years of depression, weight gain and loneliness, but they were also the power that brought me my successes. This paradox is why we must learn to recognize and control our emotions.

While I don't speak much of these dark years, I feel it's important to point out that my emotions were directly linked to the passions which were working against me. Once I harnessed my passions, everything in my life changed for the better.

This started to happen when I met my wife. Over the next decade, I started to see the power of my emotions and my passions. I fell in love with her so deeply and rapidly that I was willing to do anything to see her happy.

She was striving to be an artist and, in my mind, I finally developed a true purpose in my life. It was to do anything to see her become successful and reach her own desires and goals.

I laid out a plan in my mind. I was going to temporarily give up on my dreams of owning a successful business until she found the success she wanted. We moved in together, and I went on the hunt for a job that could support us while this was happening. Nothing was going to stand in her way, not if I could help it. What I realize now is that I could have had both; but you'll have to read on for more about that.

By harnessing my passions for her, I ended up finding the best job I ever had as an area manager. I used this job to ensure she had little to worry about and could focus on her education. This meant setting my physical desires aside, for the most part, and working on the goal at hand. I had, for the first time in my life, harnessed my passion by using my emotions of love and sex to support a goal.

We came to a balance in all our emotions when the initial physical passion leveled off. If you can recall the opening pages of your own intimate relationships, you know what I mean! We both went to work, her to become an artist and me to support her goals. I focused my energies on her and her needs, which drove us to achieve some really great results from our combined efforts. I found happiness working for someone else and helping her to reach her goals. After all, my goals were now based on her goals. This was one of the most empowering and rewarding times in my life.

There are many examples of people who do not harness the power of their emotions. Instead, they abuse them, giving in to physical desires, either ignoring the potential of their emotions or being completely unaware of that potential. This turns positive emotions into negative ones because focusing on just physical desires is selfish and short-sighted. Some people will use their sexual emotions to conquer rather than to create. They take advantage of the emotions of love and sex and use it to control rather than uplift and support.

When it comes to making decisions, we see abuses of passion all the time. Sometimes people use their passions to make decisions rather than to fuel positive thought; this too can create negativity. When we use passion for making decisions, we are not basing those decisions on facts or clear thinking, we are basing them on emotions.

We see many people who make decisions based on their emotions. When we do this, we are not having clarity of thought because our emotions override reason. Instead of using clear thinking, we are allowing an out of control set of emotions guide us. Rather than using the rider to control our emotions, our emotions start taking control of us.

Emotions should never be the means of making decisions. In fact, they are destructive when used to make decisions because emotions cause us to not think things through, or even worse, cause us to ignore the facts based on how we feel. This line is crossed by many people every day. Check yourself regularly and ask one simple question: *Am I making this decision based on emotions or on facts?* Most people today seem to be making decisions based on how it will make them feel rather than the facts. Clarity of thought and clear decision making is the key to finding success and happiness. In the case of making decisions, passion cannot be involved.

If someone is making a statement or decision based on their own emotions or what they perceive to be someone else's emotions, ignore it. Surround yourself with those who make decisions based on facts. Even if you don't like the facts, they are still the facts and should always be considered when making decisions or developing plans.

If you replace the facts with your emotions, you are leading yourself off track. When we make decisions in a haphazard fashion without the facts being the basis of our decisions, it is certainly not advantageous to our success or happiness.

Often, we don't like the facts because the Truth sometimes hurts. The person who has harnessed their emotions is not hurt or discouraged by facts. They are instead humbled and empowered by actually having the knowledge needed.

Emotions are easy to abuse because sometimes doing what feels right isn't going to have the results you hope for. By making decisions solely based on how you feel, you are likely going to hurt someone else. Making decisions on what makes you feel good is selfish and destructive.

These abuses of emotions are the dangerous portions of our potential passions. When we fail to recognize the misuses and abuses of our own emotions, we create a world of negativity around us. This negativity can stop us from reaching our goals and living our dreams.

Many of us have or have had associates that we wouldn't trust around our partners. We know these people abuse their desires and passions, and sense that their focus is purely on themselves and their desires. We recognize that they see conquering as a means of gratification. They will take their desires, try to have what isn't theirs and destroy all that lay in their path to get it.

When we focus our emotions on a positive goal, they transmute to positive energy rather than a destructive force.

This positive energy is the fuel that can be used to reach our goals and derive pleasure from the journey.

Every setback my wife and I have overcome is a point of pride now and positive emotions that provide encouragement upon meeting the next challenge. We can actually look back and give thanks for every setback or failure we've struggled through. Setbacks become challenges to overcome and feed our positive outlook even further.

Failure to have control of your emotions is a sure path to failure and unhappiness. Most decisions should be made by first setting emotions aside. If you make decisions based on your emotions rather than having a proper perspective you may want to evaluate why you do this.

Let your Passions fuel you on your ride. Never use your emotions to make decisions. You will hear this in many different forms in this book but the messages are the same. Never make a major decision while at a low point. Low points, or valleys, are no place to decide from. There are too many negative emotions involved when you are at a low point which will cloud your judgment.

It's in these valleys of life that we make our worst decisions. Wait for the clouds to clear to have clarity of thought and make your decisions when you are emotionally positive. Failure to do this can lead us to overall failure. It's in these moments that we choose to fail.

When you persevere through hard times, it's usually your passions that help fuel that perseverance. This is why passion must be in the middle of everything. It must be harnessed and controlled because it is both powerful and capable of aiding you in reaching any goal, or destroying you if you choose. By having the mental image of passion being a tool towards your goals, but not the source of your goals, you help harness its power to help you reach those goals.

Persistence

THE THIRD HORSE IS PERSISTENCE (PERSEVERANCE)

Persistence and perseverance are your final horse. Persistence never allows anything working with it to give up and accept failure. You will know no failure, nor encounter any obstacles of which you cannot conquer. Without persistence, nothing of true value is ever achieved.

When our perseverance is weakened and needs more strength to continue moving forward, we can draw upon its counterparts, passion (for strength) and desire (for guidance). Having persistence means we never stop moving forward, even when weakened. It is our power of persistence and our ability to persevere that gets us through the struggles and obstacles that will present themselves.

It is inevitable that persistence will be needed as life has a way of placing challenges and obstacles in our path. After all, no goal is ever achieved without first passing through the valleys of life and climbing over the obstacles laid before us. Persistence is your strength to persevere through setbacks. It provides the foundations for success and many of the learning tools needed to grow and succeed.

Your power of persistence responds best to trust. Persistence requires that you trust in your ability to find your way around the obstacles in life. By trusting that your persistence will pay off, you will know that any obstacle can be overcome. The power of persistence lays in your ability to trust it will prevail. Once you have this trust and understand that persistence is the manifestation of your own grit and determination **is when you become powerful**.

There is no obstacle, setback, failure or any negative influence that can deter persistence. When you imagine persistence in your mind, look see nothing but success and achievement. Perseverance draws upon desires and passions to create confidence in reaching your goals. Failure to depend on your power of perseverance and trust in your persistence can lead to your ultimate failure.

The story of my wife and the story of my journey to become an Aviation Electrician are both stories of harnessing the power of perseverance. In all great successes and triumphs, we will find persistence leading the way. Perseverance is the strength to endure; this can be seen regularly in athletes who excel and reach the highest levels of success in their relative sports. Persistence is found in nearly every story you will ever find of great success.

We find her in the most inspirational stories. She's always there, pushing the person to go one step further. If you can depend on and trust her, she guides you to success by refusing to accept failure.

Everyone has a story of perseverance, but few actually harness the lessons taught by it. Review your life as far back as you can. You will find a time in your own life that you harnessed the power of persistence. Persistence is found everywhere and in everything that is ever accomplished.

Persistence always pays dividends when you put your trust in it. Perseverance is the greater side of persistence and the greater the goal you have the more you will need to build your perseverance to succeed at it. Persistence is a large part of your inner strength, enabling you to find your way through any adversity.

Using your persistence will allow you to understand that a setback is just a setback, but failure is a choice. Persistence and perseverance prevents you from choosing failure when you are only moments away from success.

Here is another story to illustrate the power of persistence: I once met a valet who would one day become a doctor. This man's name was Tony. He was born and raised in a tough, crime-ridden neighborhood full of violence, drugs, and prostitutes. At the time, he worked for me as a valet. I liked this young man for his loyalty and hard work. One day, he came to me and asked me if he could be a supervisor. He was obviously ambitious and I like it when people have the fortitude of character to ask for what it is they want and how to achieve it.

"I don't know, can you?" I said. He wasn't ready for this response and stared at me for a moment, puzzled.

"I only ask you if you can be because I don't know what you are capable of. Only you know that."

He smiled with a great confidence. *"I would be the best."*

Now, this was impressive. He only needed a little nudge and he was already confident in his own abilities. I had taken notice of him before. He was financially responsible and was often reading when I saw him. He was polite and provided excellent customer service. He went the extra mile every chance he could. I was continually impressed by him, his work ethic and ability to learn.

"There are no supervisor positions available," I told him.

His face dropped.

"However, there are always opportunities when the next position becomes available. If you're willing to learn the job now without being concerned about the pay, I will make you first on my list since no one else is showing any initiative at this moment. You will have to prove you can do the job and show me that you're capable, not only of the paperwork, but also the people skills I require my supervisors to have."

He immediately asked without a moment's hesitation what he could do first. He spent that day learning how to do the supervisors job. The current supervisor began teaching him everything he knew. This way, he would be prepared when the job opened up.

"What do you plan to do, replace me?" The supervisor later jokingly asked me.

"No, but if you don't have a suitable replacement I can't promote you."

At the time, the company was in the middle of negotiations for two large garages. If we obtained those locations, they would both need managers. Neither of them knew this, but they were my first choices for the open positions. I simply wanted to see if they had the drive and determination to earn those positions.

We didn't get the garages, however; I was very disappointed. My valet, who was now trained and ready to be a supervisor, later came to me and asked if there was going to be any opening positions soon. I told him I didn't know, informing him of the garages which didn't come through. He then said to me that he wanted to be a nurse.

"A nurse?" I asked. This was a major shift in goals.

"Yes, a nurse. Why, do you think it's silly?" He responded.

"No, I don't. I'm just curious as to why."

His response was priceless. *"I want to make something of my life. I want to move my mother out of the hood. The only reason I stay there is to make sure nothing happens to her. I want to be able to afford a house in an area like where you live. She deserves better than what she has."*

His mother worked two jobs and raised several kids on her own. Now grown, her son worked two jobs and had just vowed to make something of his life. I explained to him that if he was going to do this, he was going to face some challenges. Nevertheless, he could become a nurse if he put his mind to it.

I looked up some of the programs for people in his position and soon found a program that would pay for his school. One afternoon after he was off work, we went to an organization that helped young African American people find funding for school. A short time later he was approved for funding and started local evening classes for nursing.

Tony eventually left the job as a valet to focus on school. He stopped in several times over the next year to keep me up to date on his progress. Here is a man who had to persevere through some serious challenges. One time he approached me ready to give up his schooling.

"Is that want you want to be, a failure?" I asked him.

His eyes scowled at me. *"I'm no failure and you know it."*

"Then prove it and finish what you started, or don't you appreciate the opportunity?"

He was getting angry now; I thought he might punch me in the face the way he swelled up and stared at me. He didn't, though. He actually conceded after realizing my intent was simple: I just wanted to help him.

"Look, I like you. You're a good man and you can do this. Don't stop because it feels like you won't be able to finish. That's when you're closest to winning."

At the time, I hadn't yet heard the philosophies about persistence. They had just come naturally to me from personal experience. My previous life experience, especially my journey years to become an Aviation Electrician and going from homeless to a business owner, had demonstrated that giving up was quitting. This young man also learned this while he trained as a supervisor.

Tony had developed a goal and stuck to it. He harnessed his passion to help his mother and followed through by persevering through the hard times all his life. He was no quitter, so there was no way if he stayed focused on his goals that he could fail. Everything he was doing was realistic and well planned. He had harnessed his power and was using it to change his life.

Several years later, I ran into him and he told me he wasn't going to be a nurse. I immediately felt horrible because I hadn't seen him and he hadn't given up yet the last time I had seen him.

"I'm in medical school. I'm going to be a doctor," he smiled and told me.

"Why the change?" I asked, feeling much better.

"I figured if I was going to put all that time and effort in, I might as well go for a bigger goal."

We shook hands and I congratulated him on his success. There was no doubt in my mind, or his, that he was going to be a doctor. The last I saw him he was doing his internship. He was one of the top students in his medical school. He had found success!

With each challenge, this man raised the bar. He didn't fear setbacks or obstacles, he was thriving on them. He was seeing each challenge as a means of greater success. Here is an example of somebody who realized his own ability to persevere and succeed.

The man I ran into that day was not the one who went to nursing school. He had grown into a successful man full of confidence and drive. This man thrived on his challenges and demanded more of life. He had even excelled beyond me, I couldn't be more proud to have known him.

His story, like all others, involves the key actions and steps needed to find success and happiness. He had the desire, passion and persistence needed to go far beyond what people expect of him. This is because it doesn't matter what others think, where you come from or what people believe you're capable of. What really matters is how you feel about these things, what your plans are and your determination to achieve those plans and meet your own goals.

No matter how many times you fail, no matter the setback, in the end it is up to you to push forward. Develop a means of failing forward and you will develop the perseverance to succeed. When you fail forward you actually don't fail, you learn from your mistake, allowing it to strengthen you. It's just another way of saying you refuse to actually fail. Instead, you learn, grow and develop even more persistence in reaching your goals.

The Reigns

FAITH & TRUST

Faith and trust are important factors in having a successful mindset. They are the Reigns by which you harness your desires, passion and perseverance. While we will discuss many aspects of the successful mindset later, having faith and trust in your desires, passions, and persistence is necessary to reach your highest potential. There is nothing that can stop you when you guide your horses with faith and trust.

Developing faith is easy to do if you put your powers of observation to work. You can simply review your life and find things you had faith in which later came to fruition. You can find hundreds of stories that explain or mention faith in regards to reaching goals. Faith and trust are interchangeable at any moment as well as working in conjunction with one another. They do, however, have their own strong suits. For instance, trust works best with persistence and faith with desire.

It's important to attach faith to your desires, having faith that they will become your reality. Trust in your persistence and perseverance to lead you through all adversity. While the horses are the means by which we achieve all things, having faith and trust in all of them is the glue that holds it together.

Since I envision faith and trust as the reigns, I envision in my mind their effect on all aspects of my purpose and goals. They are the foundations that guide our journey through life. Without them, there is a weakness in direction and a lack of guidance as well as the inability to see past the adversities and harness our own powers. Faith and trust are additional keys that allow us to find the strength needed to succeed and find happiness.

Faith and trust are part of your connection to the universe. They allow you to believe in yourself and embrace all aspects of feeling, sight, and your sixth sense (or intuition). They allow you to be in touch with all the emotions and thoughts that drive your horses towards your destination.

If you believe that you are incapable of faith or trust, then it's time to change your mind. Faith is easy to find, it can be developed through observations. It can also be seen by examining other peoples' stories of success.

My story of becoming an Aviation Electrician was one of passion and desire, as well as faith and trust in my own abilities and the goal. By harnessing the horses of desire, passion and persistence with reigns of faith and trust, I was able to achieve something that is rarely achieved.

After hearing my story, I hope to help you find faith in your own abilities. I know you can achieve more should you put your mind to work and have faith and trust in yourself, the laws of nature and the universe that supports you. Simply knowing that it can be done isn't enough. You have to believe it with no reservations. Having examples from both other's lives and your own is what truly builds a foundation of faith.

Through simple observation, faith and trust can be found working for all those who succeed, even when they don't realize it. Trust is easy to find after faith is established within your mind, it builds faith in yourself, faith in the universe, and faith in the laws of nature, all of which are guiding you towards your goals.

Examine your life carefully, looking for the moments of faith that brought you what it was you were seeking. Seek out the times in your past where you just knew something was going to happen and it did. My wife's faith in her goal to become an artist came naturally to her. She was harnessing the horses that required faith and inspired it within her. She just knew, with blind faith, what it was she wanted to be and moved forward, letting the opportunities come to her.

> *"You have it in you to develop faith in both yourself and the universe."*

When you plant a seed in the ground and it grows, you had to have had faith that it would grow. Otherwise you would not have spent the time planting it. Bees collect pollen knowing that it will become honey. The laws of nature allow you to have faith in nature if you simply take the time to observe them. The laws of success will allow you to have faith in them also. Why would the laws of nature and success apply to everything and everyone except you? They don't. They apply to you no differently then they apply to everything else. The laws of success are developed and extracted from the laws of nature.

When you start to explore this philosophy, you will begin to find more and more reasons to have faith in it. Find others who tell their stories of success, and you will find faith. In almost every case, you will find the Three Horses also. No one achieves anything without first applying the powers of their mind.

I find that there are more reasons to have faith then there are to not have it. One story after another can show you how this philosophy works and has consistently worked over the oceans of time. While much of this may seem esoteric in nature it is still quantifiable through observation.

Nearly every story of greatness reinforces the philosophy and should be a building block of having faith in it. By taking the time to not just study the philosophy but study those who are successful in whatever it is they choose to do, you will find reasons to have faith in your own powers.

When you see people who practice all or parts of the philosophy finding some form of success, you will start to build your trust in it. Once the trust is there, the faith comes very easily. The reverse is true also, faith builds trust and trust aids in finding faith.

Faith is not an abstract word or idea that you have to have some magical belief system to obtain. It's there for anyone willing to see the results of it and then realize they can also have similar results themselves. This is how we find faith.

When you trust in yourself, you can harness the powers of your own mind and utilize the powers of Desire, Passion and Persistence. Your mind will go to work for you and never stop, provided you have faith. With each new accomplishment, your faith and trust will grow and you will strengthen your persistence. This is why I say the little wins are important; they provide the foundation of continued faith.

Trust and faith are the link between you and your power. Without them, you're simply dragging along, hoping, rather than doing, and wishing rather than receiving. The two reigns you hold on to are the means by which you control yourself. Believing in yourself allows you to harness your own mind and apply that power to all that is around you.

Have faith and trust in yourself, your purpose, and your goals. Use faith and trust to make the adjustments in your path, knowing that those adjustments will eventually lead you in the right direction.

Having faith in your destination and trust in your path is much like using a navigation device when traveling. The device is useless until you put in an address (which in our case is our goals). Guiding you to the destination becomes the purpose of that device, and you put your trust in the device. Why not have these same trusts in the laws of nature and the universe?

While you may not know your actual path, by following the direction shown and adjusting your path as you are directed to, you will reach your destination. This is no different than what we do when trying to reach our own goals in life. Many of us just don't realize we are receiving the opportunities to achieve our goals because we don't have faith in those goals.

We program our minds with the destination, or in this case, our purpose or goals. We then take actions, just like turning on your GPS device and pressing "go". Then we take more actions by following the path given by the device. In life, these are the opportunities laid before us. We put our faith and trust in the device to deliver us to our final destination. Have that same faith and trust in yourself and the universe and you will reach your goals.

The GPS device is much like life; it requires all the same things to reach a goal that you do. It will deliver you to your destination, much how you can find your own path in life. The GPS follows the same rules in guidance that the universe offers you, take advantage of them and use them.

Take the actions needed to reach your destination and put your faith and trust in both the received opportunities and the path adjustments that present themselves. When we do all these things, we are in the end delivered to our goals.

By practicing faith, you will learn to spot the opportunities that will lead to your goals. If you can put faith and trust in a mechanical device, putting those beliefs to use in the laws of the universe should be easy. Hold the reins with confidence and use them to guide your path. You will eventually find your way past every obstacle.

"Have Faith that the rules of the Universe will deliver the results you want."

The Wheels

MINOR GOALS

The wheels are comprised of your minor goals. These are the smaller goals that lead to achieving your major purpose and goals in life. While the wheels may seem unimportant, they are extremely necessary for creating the steps by which we reach our goal. The wheels are the means by which you reach your major goals and purpose. There is no journey without taking those smaller first steps towards the greater goal.

The wheels are the means by which we keep moving forward, but **all your goals and dreams must be realistic.** Realistic goals coincide with the laws of nature and must be adhered to. You cannot be a star athlete if your knees are damaged any more than you can be a doctor without having gone to medical school. Always play to your strengths. They are your strengths for a reason; you may just not know what that is yet.

Minor goals help us grow and gain practical experience and knowledge so that we will be ready when the greater opportunities present themselves. When we reach each goal, we should set the next goal higher. By starting small, keeping our eyes and minds open and ready to recognize opportunity when it presents itself the opportunities around us will become more apparent and easier to recognize.

Many of us may not know what our major purpose is. However, by setting minor goals and purposes we will eventually discover our major purpose and then strive for it. In my individual case, I set my major purpose very high. You should do the same! When you do this, you will achieve more because your goals are set so high.

To start reaching my goals, I had to set them first no differently then you need to set yours. My goal was to own enough real estate so that my wife and I will only work because we enjoy what we are doing. I thought this was my major purpose. After all, I set the goal, so it must be my purpose, right? Wrong. My major purpose was suggested to me later by my own coach and mentor. This created opportunities to live out my life's dream. These opportunities presented themselves and even led to this book. Becoming a personal improvement trainer and coach are further evidence of the opportunities that presented themselves and lined up with my life's dream. You can have these same experiences but you must start somewhere or you can never move forward.

I had always wanted to be a writer and wrote a lot of manuscripts, primarily focused on helping people by describing my own life's experiences. I had also written a book on Quantum Spirituality, which was inspired by Amit Goswami and his series of books about quantum consciousness, most notably *The Self-Aware Universe*.

I also wrote a book on how to become a manager and be the best in your company by using interpersonal skills and going the extra mile, which was titled *So You Want to Be in Management*. My wife and I also self published a book called *Owning Chickens*, which was a fun project. I wrote it and she did the editing and illustrations. We never sold a copy and I didn't care, I just enjoyed the writing.

My first goal in real estate was to get my first deal in the first two months. I had no doubt that I was going to be successful. To my gratitude, we wrote the first contract six weeks into my training, and we closed the deal a few weeks later. My next goal was to find a student whom I could bring in so that they could help us run our business by learning first-hand every aspect that we could teach him or her about buying and selling real estate. Their pay would be based on performance, and would be generous.

We knew most people would not want a job like that. After all, most people don't want to be paid on performance. They want hourly wages because they get the false feeling of security from being on payroll. Thankfully, we found a person and trained him to help run the business while making a lot of money doing it. As this is written, this individual is still training and working hard.

During these opening successes, an opportunity presented itself and my ambitions to be a writer and life coach came back. Through a strange set of circumstances, the next moment I was both a real estate investor and life coach, all while working on my first book. I quickly received three students and made contacts that would lead me to actually living out my dream.

I had set the goal to become a real estate investor. This led me to setting minor goals. I read books, studied real estate investing and became knowledgeable in real estate. After meeting those goals, I sought out a real estate coach, who then became my personal coach. I then started looking for properties to buy. This led to my first investment property. During this time, I started working on becoming a coach myself. Each little step led to greater opportunities. Each little goal was building up towards achieving my greater goals.

The wheels are important because they are carrying you towards your destination and lift you above the ground. They also keep you from dragging or slowing down. When you have a true major purpose all the smaller goals help you get there.

Your minor goals should also help others along the way. The idea of paying it forward comes to mind. By being conscious of the need to help others you will be able to develop the plans, find partners, obtain the finances, and reach all goals necessary to achieve your greater goals.

As I stated much earlier in this book, you must use the philosophy to master it. Everything needs to work together in harmony. While having small portions will elevate you, true success is guaranteed when you have all of it.

The wheels are important as it's the minor goals that lead to the largest successes and you must be conscious of this. Never underestimate the need to have minor goals. Each goal is striving towards the larger goal and no one will reach their greatest goals instantly. You must plant the seed, let it germinate and then nurture it to maturity. Failure to do so will end in failure. You cannot harvest fruit from trees that have not had the opportunity to grow and mature.

Here is a good example of this: you may want to get an education about whatever it is you are trying to achieve. So, you set the minor goal to educate yourself first. Once you achieve this goal, you can move forward towards your larger goals by applying that new knowledge. Each step is a minor goal with the bigger goal in mind. These minor goals are the wheels carrying you towards your greater goals.

When you work towards a new goal, all these minor goals are the wheels on your chariot allowing it to continue to move forward. They provide the foundations to keep moving forward; as each goal is achieved it must be immediately replaced with a new goal. For me, many of these minor goals have been self-education, gaining of experience and learning the lessons life has to offer.

I use minor goals to achieve the smaller things I want to achieve. I set goals to read a certain amount each week to expand my education. Accordingly, I plan my day early and a set minor goal to reach every morning. This is the "three actions a day" policy. We will cover more of this in the Taking Actions section of this book.

When you set minor goals and focus the powers of your mind on them, you will achieve them. Achieving minor goals equates to small wins and having a successful winning day. With each successful day and each small win, we become more focused and our lives become more fulfilling. We also develop more faith in ourselves and our goals.

These small wins all have a positive effect on both our emotional levels and fulfillment in life. The more of these minor goals you reach, the more positive you will be.

The size of these goals can vary from very small to rather large, yet fall short of your major goals or purpose. When that major goal is reached you will know it, the minor goals are merely the path to your major ones. They are, however, key in reaching that goal and recognizing the opportunities to move forward towards that goal. No one will achieve that greater goal without first achieving the smaller ones.

Pile up your little wins, build your faith and confidence and use your minor goals to create balance in your life. With every minor goal reached, you are one step closer to your major goals. With each small win, you build a greater foundation for success.

Many people see the small victories as insignificant. In reality, they are not insignificant by any standard. They are the means by which you move forward, improve your life, find happiness, and reach your greater goals.

What may seem like a major goal today may actually be a minor goal in a larger picture that you are just not aware of yet. Having a college degree may seem like the means to a successful career, when in reality, it is only one of the wheels in getting you there. College teaches you the basics and gives you the knowledge you need, and experience gives you the means to apply that knowledge, while this philosophy gives you the path to achieve your goals.

It is up to you to actually do the work, find the job, start the business, or simply grow your career. Hindsight shows us what major goals we had that were actually only minor goals. Having value in each one of these wins and successes is necessary to grow the inner-self to expand into greater areas of life. Plant the seed, nurture its growth and aid it to maturity. Only then can you harvest the fruit of your labors.

The Sixth Sense

SEEING OPPORTUNITY & RECOGNIZING INSPIRATION

The sixth sense is that of intuition and inspiration. Without it, the road to reaching our goals is longer and much harder. The woods are thicker and more difficult to traverse if we don't understand our sixth sense. While it takes faith to master it, this is a skill you can develop with practice. It is up to you to develop this skill.

We must learn to harness our sixth sense, for it is a communication from the universe which feeds our goals. For some it's a difficult idea to grasp, believing there is some esoteric magic to it of which they don't possess. Others find that it comes naturally because they embrace it. Those who easily find it embrace their intuitions with confidence.

The universe speaks to us constantly. When listening to the universe, we must put faith into something outside of ourselves. Many people will put their own desires or ambitions above it, and accordingly, ignore warnings and miss opportunities that the sixth sense provides. In order to use our sixth sense, we must have the flexibility to change directions when the time is right.

Harnessing the sixth sense may sound difficult, but it can be done. Just pay attention. We hear stories all the time where people could feel that they were in a bad situation but ignored the feelings. These are the ones who typically get into some kind of trouble. You may also hear things such as: *"I had that idea also. He got rich with, it while I didn't. "*

Here is an example of my own sixth sense and how it helped me complete this book: Over my life I have written many books, none of which were ever published other than the aforementioned self published flop *Owning Chickens.*

After embracing the philosophies of success and studying them more and more, I wanted to start teaching others. Suddenly, the urge to write a book came back. The universe would play a greater role in my decision to pursue these dreams and turn them into greater goals than I ever thought possible. I had read about mastering the sixth sense in many previous books, both in my esoteric and philosophical studies. I believed in it and tended to follow my instincts regularly.

When I met my new coach and had my first private lesson, he asked about my writing. I mentioned that I had written a few manuscripts but never published anything. (Of course, this was excluding the self-published *Owning Chickens*).

He immediately asked me why I wasn't coaching and instructed me to finish publishing a book. I don't know if he realized what he had just done, but he lit a fire in me. This fueled my lifelong desire to be a writer and coach. In the past I had limiting thoughts and beliefs that stopped me, but they were gone now and I was ready to move forward.

All of a sudden, the money I wanted to make in real estate was less important than pursuing my dreams of being a writer and coach. I would now have to take a dream, develop a plan, and turn the dream into a goal. Dreams mean nothing without a plan to achieve them. Once you have a plan they become a goal. Once you have a goal, you have something to take action on. The key is to have your goal planned out. This is also referred to as intention setting.

I would make becoming a coach, author and trainer one of my wheels, with real estate on the other side allowing my major goal to become reality. I would be striving for this goal and at the same time living out my dreams.

My fear of writing in the past was based on my own internal beliefs that I couldn't be a writer because I was a poor English student. Now I know that I don't need to be excellent in English to be a writer. The resources, the people, are out there who can help me along the way. I can simply seek out a co-author or editor to correct my errors and still tell my story. My problem was solved by the action of hiring my weaknesses and playing to my strengths.

My new coach, without even having realized it, opened a door in my mind. I had my major purpose set and was using real estate to achieve it. However, real estate wasn't my lifelong dream; it was a means of building wealth to reach my goals of financial freedom. I just wanted to be a writer and teacher or life-coach, but I never saw the right path before now. Following the philosophies, I started asking for it from the universe; it was in my mind constantly and it was about to be given to me.

Pay close attention as this bit is important. I began to ask regularly, not in the form of a prayer, but in the form of requesting guidance. Once I did this my dream became a goal, and I actively sought out a path and created a plan. I began to take actions on that plan. The first step was to ask for guidance and be ready to receive it in the form of inspirations.

Once the decision was made, I began asking the universe for guidance. I dwelled on this thought while I was meditating before going to sleep each night. I wanted to find the inspiration needed so I could start moving towards my new goal.

The following morning a thought came to me: The Three Horses that lead to success are *Desire, Passion* and *Persistence*…a philosophy started to form in my mind! This just came out me while on the phone with a coaching student. The entire overview of the philosophy was there, just waiting to be tapped. Once I started to relax and write, it began to flow out of me easily.

Everything I had learned about the philosophies of success was now being drawn into one concise thought. A unique view was coming into my mind. Each night a little more came to me, and suddenly a new perspective of the philosophies was formed in my creative mind. Not only was it flowing into my mind, it was being embedded. The reasons for each step and each section of the philosophy seemed to just *be there*. I needed to only review my life and do some serious self-evaluation to find every aspect of the philosophy in action.

The Three Horses flowed into me through one creative thought after another. After discussing it with my wife and others, it received great feedback and seemed to resonate with people in a very positive way. Each person loved it, so I proposed it to strangers to receive more critical reviews. These people not only liked it, but they wanted me to repeat it so that they could write it down. There was nothing new about this philosophy --it simply was a new interpretation of my life and the books I've read, which I still study to this day.

I began to see the Three Horses not only in my own life, but in every inspirational story of success and triumph over adversity. They were there every time; the philosophy was so obvious to me now. It became a part of me, and during my own meditations, I began to realize how much of it I had applied and what parts were missing. It was the foundation for this book. My creative mind was delivering to me exactly what I was asking for. It was my sixth sense in action, working with the unseen forces around me to help me develop the philosophy you are now reading.

With each pass over the text, a new understanding or another leg of my philosophy was born. As Napoleon Hill once said:

"More gold has been mined from the minds of men than ever from the earth."

A good friend of mine loved this philosophy and supported every step of it. He continually confirmed that this idea would strike gold. My mind was the mine and the universe provided the golden ore. The golden ore was the inspirations, and the philosophy itself the guide, helping me to lay out this very book and realize the success I would find from it.

My sixth sense was in full swing now. It was delivering to me each step I needed to take, guiding my writings and allowing me to see beyond what I had learned and into the deeper meanings.

What before had taken months of work was now flowing out rapidly. I could barely believe it. I hadn't been writing for longer than two weeks and suddenly I had a base manuscript from which to work on; one that even my wife was impressed with. She would later help me when adversity arrived, right on schedule, threatening the completion of the book.

In my readings and my associations, I learned that you can always bring someone else in to improve what you're working on. Developing a partnership was the next intuition I had. Only a few days later, the opportunity to meet some of the top writers and speakers on the topic was given to me. My sixth sense was telling me to jump on the opportunity. *Make this happen* came into my head. I prepared for it like nothing I have ever prepared for.

The universe did more than just help me find and form the idea; it was reinforcing it on a regular basis, encouraging me to continue on this path. One incredible example: one day in the mail I received a catalog addressed to me for horse products. This included items such as food, bridles, shoes, and so on. I had never in my life ordered anything for horses. I don't know how they found my name or why they mailed it, but I didn't miss the hint. To this day I have not yet received another catalog, just the one, the one time, and it sits on my shelf as a testament to the validity of the philosophies. It was the universe speaking to me; I needed only recognize the message. That message? The Three Horses were my key to success. This metaphor was going to provide me the gateway to finding success in being a trainer, a coach, a teacher, and helping to make other's lives better.

Strangely, this wasn't the only hint that was going to come to me. I had asked my wife to put together a logo for my new company and I wanted it to be Three Horses coming at the viewer. She had completed a mural in the past that involved horses and I knew that she could use that as a guide.

The following weekend, my wife and I went out on our routine trip to the flea market. This is where we buy fresh veggies, food, and find neat stuff for the house. Out of nowhere, she stumbled upon a box of books, and they were all on horse anatomy. If you're unaware, artists occasionally use anatomy books to help develop the proper perspectives when drawing out new art.

The seller didn't normally have books, but he had come across these and put them out for sale, stacked in an unassuming box on the ground. She had been attracted to the box, and it provided her with exactly what she was looking for: books on horse anatomy that would help her develop my logo and cover work for the book.

If you are open to the sixth sense, you will realize that these seeming coincidences were lining up to help me realize my goals. It's our sixth sense that recognizes this as more than just coincidence.

This wasn't the end though, there was more to come. We had been ordering some hardcovers of some of my favorite books, the same ones that helped solidify the Three Horse Philosophy. I was ordering books from people who, through their writings, were my teachers -- authors whose teachings are important to me. The books started showing up signed, as mentioned before. To me, this was another confirmation of my new direction.

Even this wasn't it though. In the same span of time, I was also invited to meet a group of speakers, trainers, millionaires, entrepreneurs, writers, and publishers at a special event. I saw this as the biggest opportunity of my life ever laid down before me. The people I was going to spend the week with were some of the biggest names in the motivational and coaching industries.

To top it off, I was invited personally to attend the event by its organizer. Since he was friends with one of my mentors, my efforts to surround myself with like-minded people were proving to be profitable. While this profit wasn't necessarily monetary, it was extremely valuable in many other ways. I now had support from people who had succeeded in exactly what it was I wanted to do. Opportunities were presenting themselves quickly and I now had new friends who could give me the guidance needed to become successful in what I was doing.

In my mind, everything was lining up. All that was necessary now was to recognize the opportunities as they presented themselves and seize my moments.

When we are learning to recognize our sixth sense, we need to do a lot of self evaluation. Learning to recognize warnings is a good way to start learning to recognize your sixth sense. Once you recognize it, you will start to be able to distinguish between what is sixth sense and what is only thought. Thoughts can come in the form of worry, stress, and other negative emotions.

This is one reason why we want to try to eliminate worry and fear from our lives. They cloud your ability to recognize your sixth sense. This cloudy internal vision lowers our ability to recognize the intuitions being sent to us from our sixth sense.

Even upon gaining experience with developing your sixth sense, try to always consciously evaluate it. The more times we evaluate what was intuition and what wasn't, we begin to understand it more clearly. We can then apply intuition and validate it through clear thinking. When we do these continual self evaluations, we learn to make those critical distinctions between worry, fear and genuine intuitions that lead to recognizing opportunity and seizing the moment.

In many cases, we are given the inspirations to draw up a plan to achieve our goals but ignore them or don't recognize them. Another mistake that people make is to attempt to rationalize their intuitions by asking others about their idea.

Unless you have a completely supportive group around you, this may be something to avoid.

Your intuition is yours; no one else can evaluate it for you. Supportive people, however, can provide a foundation of support so that you can validate or embrace your intuitions. It's still yours and yours alone to decide on. You can use clear thinking (which we will discuss shortly) to validate it.

Many people think that you have to get lucky in order to be successful. In reality, there is little luck involved in any of this. By learning to recognize an intuition or inspiration, we can then take positive actions to realize our goals. People who seem to be getting lucky are, whether they realize it or not, actually taking advantage of their sixth sense and taking action on it.

Combined with belief and faith, they move and take actions when opportunities present themselves. They are putting themselves in the way of opportunity and seizing their moments. They recognize those moments through the use of their sixth sense.

If there is no sixth sense or intuition, you're left only with your ability of reasoning and logic. You can use this to apply clear thinking to the situation. However, using your faculty of reasoning combined with the power of intuition is an extremely powerful means of finding success. Recognizing when the universe is talking to you and trying to help you move forward is key to creating harmony with all aspects of your mind and abilities. Your sixth sense is like a beacon leading the way, you need only look for it to find it and put it to use.

Once you can clear up the negative and find the positive you will build faith, recognize your sixth sense, and be able to manage yourself far better. Do your best to turn everything into a positive and embrace your sixth sense. It may take some practice to build faith in it and learn how to recognize it, but I know you can if you try.

Clear Thinking

BETTER DECISIONS AND CONQUERING THE CHALLENGES

Clear thinking is important to personal improvement and success. Without it, you are basing your decisions on something other than facts. As mentioned in the sixth sense section, we can use the sixth sense to spot an opportunity. We can then use clear thinking to evaluate and decide whether or not to take advantage of that opportunity.

Thinking clearly is an artform that can be mastered with a little practice. This heavily contrasts with the way that many people come to decisions today; if you are basing your decision making on the opinions of others, you are not practicing clear thinking. If you are basing decisions on your emotions or how you feel about the situation, again you are not thinking clearly.

To think clearly is to evaluate the situation from all angles, learn the facts from all sides and apply that to your decision-making process. Along with your sixth sense, clear thinking works in conjunction with the opportunities that are presented when you harness your desires.

Therefore, when you use your sixth sense to spot an opportunity, you can check its viability and validity by applying clear thinking. Clear thinking should be used in any decision-making process.

Making assumptions without the facts is the mother of all mistakes. Don't assume things, instead, start obtaining the facts. When you make a decision, you should base that decision on all the available facts you can come up with. When you are lacking in facts, do not rely on emotion to make the decision. Instead, rely on your reasoning to attempt to extrapolate the best logical conclusion.

Clear thinking is key to leadership and excellent decision-making. When you have a set of reasons for your actions, people are more likely to follow and support you. By being a good decision-maker and standing behind a decision, you will have more confidence when it comes time to make the call and back up your decision. You will have more confidence in your own decisions when making them if you have the facts and reasoning worked out beforehand. People who practice clear and independent thinking are not easily controlled. They do not buy a story simply because they are told a story. They evaluate it, find the facts from all sides, and make clear decisions about it. When you use clear thinking, you are not part of a pack. You will be elevating yourself above the pack.

Use clear thinking to make your own decisions and you may find that your life is under your control. By allowing other people to make decisions for us, and failing to find out the facts, we are actually wandering through life like a lemming. Lemmings follow the leader, even off a cliff, so don't be one. Think for yourself and make informed decisions.

Making decisions based on facts gives you confidence while reducing fear, worry and anxiety. It allows you to project a positive attitude about your decision. It also gives you the ability to explain yourself clearly and concisely when needed.

While the universe may give us intuition, we should always validate it with as many facts as possible. Those who think for themselves are powerful individuals. *Do you think for yourself or do you allow others to think for you?*

Once you start practicing clear thinking, you can use this to validate the intuition or inspiration that comes to you from your sixth sense and you can move forward with more confidence. Since confidence is key to achieving your goals, clear thinking is important because it is the key to having confidence.

To cite an example from my own personal experience on this topic: I used education to create knowledge to then make clear decisions about what it was I was going to do. Let's briefly discuss my inspiration to become a real estate investor.

When I first had the idea, it was clear that real estate was an excellent investment vehicle. I just didn't know how to start. The inspiration to become a real estate investor was the catalyst which led me into professional coaching, training and writing. This is not how it began though, or how I expected it to go.

I initially decided to just focus on real estate. During this time, however, I also began studying the philosophies of success. I would need to understand the methods by which real estate moguls acquired their fortunes. This, of course, was in addition to all the other information I could possibly find on the topic. Owning a single house wouldn't cut it, and I knew this.

My intuition to study both real estate and the philosophies on success were spot on. This was, however, after ignoring the desire to read the philosophies for years. I had convinced myself they would be boring and that I could figure it out on my own. Well, I was wrong. Once I gave in and followed the urge (my inspiration) to study those philosophies, they were much more exciting and exhilarating than I imagined. They gave me the knowledge to make informed decisions.

Through this journey, the experience also led me to a mentor -- almost no one of notable success did it without first having some form of mentor or coach. This was the best decision of my life and has led to all the success I now enjoy today. Using the rules of clear thinking and good decision making, based on all the facts available, will allow you to make good decisions. The likelihood of making mistakes is reduced when you apply some clear thinking to your decision making. This is also the key to mitigating risk and reducing liability in both your life and business.

An example of using clear thinking when making a decision:

Imagine you own a business that makes custom built oak desks for exclusive clients. Let's say that you have 5 days to finish and deliver an order for a desk. The product requires 2 men to build. However, you can't put any more people on the job because there is no space or available employees. It will take 36 hours to complete the project (or 72 man-hours).

Your workers work 8 hours a day. It will take three days for the product to arrive once shipped and three days to build, therefore the desk will not arrive on time because it's going to take six days to finish and ship. In this situation, the regular 8-hour work day will not be suitable. The desk is going to take too long to finish and it will arrive late after shipping time. So, you have to either choose to deliver the product late or have the employees work overtime. Either of these will cause you a reduction in profit and/or problems with customers.

What is the best thing to do in this situation? You don't want to reduce your profit line, but you also don't want to upset the customer. You decide to get the facts before deciding by calling the customer.

After doing the math, you see that a 5% discount is only 25% of what it would have cost to pay employees overtime. In other word's it will cost you three times more to pay the overtime then offer a discount. You decide to call the customer and offer the discount rather than paying the overtime.

You call the customer and explain that you can get the desk out on time or that you can offer the customer a 5% discount if they can wait a few extra days. The customer informs you that they will accept the 5% discount and this retains much of your original profit line. This also makes the customer feel appreciated, because you cared enough to call them and explain what was going on.

You have made a clear-thinking decision about this situation. You found out all the facts and kept the costs down, profits up all while ensuring the customer is happy.

If you had made the decision to ship it late without the informing the customer, the customer likely would have been upset with your company. If you simply made the decision to have the employees work overtime and get the product out on time it would have cost you more of your profit line.

Clear thinking and knowing the facts is important if you want to make a decision about anything. This concept should apply to all the decisions you make.

When someone tells you a story and it involves another person, don't automatically take their word for it. Try to remember that each person has their own perspective. While neither may be lying, their view of the situation is uniquely biased by their own beliefs and perspectives.

Don't merely accept one side over the other just because you feel they are telling the truth. The truth is a matter of internal belief by the person telling the story. While both involved may have similar stories, and both feel they are telling the truth, you must gather the facts before you can make a decision about the situation. This is an important aspect in leadership because when we make decisions that involve others, we must be clear on why we are making that decision.

This idea goes far beyond the simple "he said, she said" types of stories. There is a continual failure by many of us to evaluate and think clearly about a wide range of topics. We form political opinions, make financial decisions, and other major life decisions simply on the word of someone else without *"doing the homework on the topic"*.

Many of us take the word of a friend, associate or family member without checking the facts. In many instances, we may form opinions based on our emotions. We end up forming our opinion or making a decision without knowing the facts. All of these situations are caused by a failure to recognize the need for clear thinking when it comes to decision making.

If you don't possess the facts or you are unsure of them, do yourself and everyone else a favor and restrain yourself from making a decision or having an opinion on the topic. This can be difficult because, after all, many of us base most of our decisions and opinions on how we feel or on the opinions of others. We may even ignore facts when they are presented to us. Stay aware of yourself and don't be like this. When you are not in possession of the facts, others who use clear thinking can see right through you and you lose credibility.

How you present facts to people plays a larger role in whether or not you can get them to hear what you're saying. You will find that clear thinking and good decision making are beneficial to you and those around you. Examining others statements and finding out what they are basing their opinions on will quickly inform you as to whether or not to have a discussion with them or simply let it go.

Most of the time, debates are not really based on facts. In reality, they are debates based on emotions. When you get into debates based on emotions, nobody wins and everybody loses. Simply use clear thinking to find out whether you should enter into the conversation or walk away. The negativity that can be brought about by trying to have a conversation with someone who is in possession of little or no facts about a topic is simply a waste of time. If you are taking advice from someone who has no real knowledge of the topic, then you are committing to actions based on opinions rather than facts. This can lead to failure or setback that could have been avoided.

Always use clear thinking and pay attention to the times that you don't. You might find that while the results might be favorable, you're actually taking greater risks when you fail to think clearly and properly evaluate the situation.

An example of this point happened when I decided to leave my job as an Environmental Technician (a fancy name for "janitor") by putting in my two weeks' notice. Many people were curious as to what I was going to do. I was leaving to become a fulltime real estate investor. After mentioning this, there were many opinions that were given to me.

The opinions given to me were just that -- opinions -- and nothing more; not a single one of these people actually owned an investment property. Therefore, whatever they were saying meant nothing because their opinion was based on little to no facts or practical experience. When I listened to them, I realized that they were actually deriving their opinions from what someone else had told them or their own fears, which were both useless to me.

These opinions were nothing to base any kind of decision on. I'm not saying this to be cruel or belittle these people. I know they simply wanted to help. However, they didn't have the facts or experience to help. Unfortunately, this is the standard operating procedure for most people, especially those not familiar with the philosophies of success.

When you think about it, it's no better than the blind leading the blind because they had no knowledge on the topic. Yet they were ready to tell me (someone who had just spent 2.5 years studying the topic) what I should, or shouldn't, be doing.

With the guidance of my mentor, a lifelong real estate investor, a real estate investment career seemed very plausible. Once I received these opinions, I simply smiled and responded to them: *"That's interesting. I will look into it before I do something stupid."*

Of course, this was my preferred route; otherwise the alternative would be to engage them in a pointless debate. I didn't allow their lack of clear thinking to affect mine, nor did I allow their negativity on the topic to make my view negative. I thought it out and realized that they just didn't know what they were talking about; they were embracing their fears and in this case those fears were based on a lack of knowledge.

I wasn't in possession of all the facts either, but I knew this. **I knew what I didn't know.** Using clear thinking, I was able to gently back out of the conversation without the person recognizing the intent behind my actions. I didn't want to hurt their feelings or end up in a debate about the topic. My decision was made and I wasn't going to change it.

HERE ARE THE SIMPLE STEPS TO CLEAR THINKING:

1.   Ask all pertinent questions about the topic.

2.   Get all the facts available about the topic.

3.   Examine those facts and apply them to the situation.

4.   Make your decision based only on the available facts.

These simple steps are the basis to clear thinking. Sometimes it isn't easy to come to a decision because you may not know of all the facts. Regardless, these are the basic steps to analyzing the situation and thinking clearly about it.

By regularly implementing the practice of clear thinking we can begin to make better decisions and form valid opinions. Clear thinking is key to both your credibility and the validity of your decisions and opinions. Clear thinking also allows you to give counsel rather than opinions. By having real facts or experience, you can confidently and honestly give counsel and help others.

Reversing Negativity

POSITIVE MENTAL ATTITUDE &TURNING THE NEGATIVE INTO POSITIVE

Improving yourself should be a constant goal to strive for. The more we improve ourselves, the better we become at harnessing the powers of our mind. Our minds do not respond well to negativity, whether it's internal or external. Dispelling negativity, and removing it from our lives, is one of the best means of achieving happiness. Happiness, success, and negativity are all governed by our mind, not external forces. By refusing to be negative, we empower our Horses and strengthen our ability to carry on in the face of any challenge.

One of the most common negative phrases I've heard is the phrase: *"I can't"*. I'm guilty of doing it myself for much of my life. The thought you *"can't"* do something is reinforced by the words supporting that thought. This is a sure means of never doing it, no matter what "it" is.

The mere thought that *"you can't"* do something is one of the greatest self-imposed setbacks when trying to achieve anything. When you proclaim your inability to do something, you are training your subconscious to believe it.

With each declaration and proclamation of your own inabilities, you embed the negative idea into your subconscious mind. Worse yet, you project it as a desire to the universe. In turn, the universe delivers the means or feelings that help you fail or prevent you from even trying. If you truly believe you can't do something, there is no way you will ever do it.

We speak a lot about the Law of Attraction in this book, so it's important to recognize that you attract both the good and the bad to you through your own thoughts. The universe does not seem to know the differences between the good or the bad; it only knows what you want and it does all it can to deliver those desires to you.

The images and thoughts we embed into our minds that reinforce our belief that we cannot achieve something will lead us to manifest failure. I have heard people say, *"I can't leave my job or I will never get a promotion."* To their own dismay, this is exactly what happens -- they never leave their job or get that promotion. We fail to realize the power of our own thoughts and desires or how they affect our actions. Without even trying, we end up manifesting all the negative things we never wanted.

Interestingly, the idea that we can't do something is easy to accept because it requires no effort. When we say we can't do something, then achieving it isn't going to happen; no effort in making the attempt is needed. Therefore, you simply don't try and the manifestation is failure.

Additionally, if we don't want to do something, the universe helps us to avoid it by placing roadblocks in the way... preventing us from doing it. In reality, you don't want to do it. You are literally requesting failure before even trying. The power of our mind to manifest our desires is real and works both for, and against, us so be mindful of what you are thinking and what you believe. These thoughts and beliefs are tangible and can be measured by observing the results we've had because of them.

Measuring the tangibility of the thought *"I can't"* is rather easy: anything that you thought you couldn't do, you probably never tried. We often don't realize that it was the projection of the *"I can't"* thought that ensured our failure.

The same is true for the *"I can"* thought, which is also usually easy to prove. We often miss life lessons as they are given to us because they are subtle, and in many cases, just assume that's how things are supposed to go. This is why it's important to engage in things that spark our passion and desires. For when we engage in doing the things we want to do, we are sending the opposite of the "I can't" message and can therefore manifest success.

A great example that most of us can relate to is learning to ride a bike. When I learned to ride a bike, like many, I had the *"I can't"* thought come through my head before taking off the training wheels. I held to this belief until I was convinced by an outside source (my parents in this case) that I could ride my bike without training wheels. My thoughts were changed from *"I can't"* to *"I can."* The end result was me riding my bike without training wheels.

The change in thought pattern had to happen before I was able to achieve this simple childhood feat, one of which most children are very proud of. This pride is derived from overcoming the fear, such as possibly falling or getting hurt, associated with learning to ride a bike.

I eventually ended up owning a variety of motorcycles in my life, and have ridden over a million miles. If I hadn't changed my internal thought from *"I can't"* to *"I can,"* this would have never happened.

Once we have the *"I can"* thought and fixate on it, there is nothing that will stop us. As a child, I had many different bicycle accidents and lots of bruises and cuts that came from them; those adversities were overcome thanks to my persistence and perseverance, and none of them deterred the *"I can"* mindset when it came to riding my bicycle.

The *"I can"* mindset comes with a price tag of challenges. With each challenge, we grow stronger and with each setback we learn how to achieve more. Unless we are willing to pay those prices, we will never grow from our setbacks. Those prices are the effort, actions, and determination to achieve the goal.

In this case we put our desire to ride a bike to work. We have a passion to learn how, and the persistence to get through the setbacks. In almost every achievement you will find the Three Horses.

When we change our thoughts from negative ones to positive ones, we are bound to achieve those goals. The loftier the goal, the more you will need your mental horses to achieve it.

The bike story is a simple example of how your mind works in conjunction with the laws of nature. The greater the goal, the more effort it will take to achieve it. Controlling your thoughts, applying your desire, passion and persistence combined with using the reigns of faith and trust is a winning recipe. You can achieve anything you can conceive and, most importantly believe, provided those goals are realistic and within the laws of nature. Faith and trust are necessary to change the negative *"I can't"* thoughts to a new positive mindset of *"I can"*.

Changing our mindset is the first step in reaching new goals. If you want to do something new then you will first have to change the way you think. If you keep doing the same old things you will have the same old results. Your mindset about your new goals or path in life will have to be adjusted to achieving that new goal.

We have a mindset about everything in our lives and evaluating that mindset is important in understanding it. Once we understand that mindset, we can work on making it more positive, which will help us to achieve our goals.

If you believe all that you will ever make is minimum wage and the only way to make more is if someone forces your employer to pay you more, then it's likely you will be stuck in minimum wage jobs. Your mindset and internal beliefs are in control of what it is you are. By holding fast to the thought that others hold your destiny in their hands, you empower them and they control you. You are not thinking for yourself and therefore you will be unable to achieve your goals on your own.

However, if you believe you are worth more and demand more from life, then the universe will provide opportunities to have more. In the case of making money, this is a successful money mindset. Make a mental note here: the universe does not provide the end; it provides the opportunity or means to reach that end. Remember how in the chapter *The Story of My Wife*, how one person was influencing the outcome of her project? She didn't allow this to happen; it was her *"I can"* mindset that prevented outside influences from determining her success.

In my life, I have earned exactly what I thought I would earn, or at least close to it. I always have earned what I believed I was worth. In order to be successful, you must believe you are worthy of success. You must believe you are worth what you are seeking in life.

How much are you worth? Do you believe you are worth more? If so, are you seizing opportunities to have more? These are important questions that only you can answer. You must answer them honestly. If your desire is to find happiness, make more money and create success in your life, then you have to believe you can.

Knowing your limitations is different than saying *"I can't do it."* Play to your strengths and hire those who can strengthen your weaknesses. Nobody knows how to do everything. None of us hold talents in all available industries; the universe just isn't designed like that. Our passions are usually determined by what we are talented at; either that or our talents are determining our passions. In either case, these are our strengths.

If you know you can do something but it's going to take time to learn how, then this is a current weakness. You can take the time to learn about that weakness to conquer it or you can find someone to fill that gap. If learning this skill isn't necessarily needed to achieve your goal, then that time may be better spent elsewhere.

Hire or seek help from others who are good at whatever it is you are not good or skilled at. I'm not good at bookkeeping so I hire bookkeepers. I don't have time to become a lawyer so I hire lawyers. The list goes on and on. Don't get hung up on the *"I can't"* mindset. Even though you may not be able to do something, or you're not good at it, doesn't mean you can't get it done. By bringing someone in who can get it done, you move past the obstacle with ease; when you do this, you are taking the *"I can't get it done"* mindset and changing it to the *"It will get done"* mindset. You do not need to know everything. If you change your way of thinking about it and hire professionals in those areas, you can overcome these challenges with little effort.

Actors hire voice coaches if they need to learn accents or a particular way of speaking for a big role. The same idea should hold true for you. If you need to hire someone else to help you, then do it. Put your focuses where you will have the most success. You not only get the task done more efficiently, but you also build confidence in reaching and achieving whatever it is you are trying to accomplish.

Years ago, I once had all the stamina and strength in the world. I did almost everything physical on my own. Today, I hire people to do much of it for me, which saves so much time that is better spent focusing on my goals. Outsourcing gets the job done better and faster than I ever would have.

This is not saying *"I can't."* This is changing an *"I can't"* situation into an *"I can"* situation by bringing in outside help. All you need to do is admit that you need help to resolve the problem. Instead of struggling, or needing to research or learn a new task, you end up solving the problem and completing the job at hand with the help of others.

The entire idea is to not get sidetracked from your major goal or purpose. If you need a lawyer, hire one, or spend the years needed to become one. Which is wiser?

I mentioned earlier that I was a poor English student. I wanted to be a writer, even with this deficiency hanging over my own thoughts and beliefs. There was a lot of English and writing knowledge of which I was lacking. I, however, hired an editor for this book because I recognized my weakness and found a solution. I didn't take away from the time needed to write the book by becoming perfect in English. I did however have to become far more proficient then I was. I did a lot of self-study and practiced to improve my writing.

I needed an editor to ensure that my grammar was proficient and my bad spelling habits were fixed. When reading the edits, I learned from them and put those into practice immediately when writing the second draft of the book.

Years of practice writing and dozens of manuscripts, combined with the recognition that I always need to be improving, led to my ability to write this book. The editor was hired to ensure anything I wasn't proficient at was corrected. In this process, I learned even more about writing. You can do the same with just about anything it is you want to do.

I didn't let the limiting thoughts about my level of English skills stop me from what it was I wanted to do. I put my mind to it and found a way to make it happen. At the same time, I was improving my own skills. You can do the same thing by believing you can.

Here is another story, the perfect example of bringing in others to help you solve your weaknesses. This one is about a man who has polio and has ended up living in an iron lung. His name is Paul Alexander; he wanted to do something with his life -- he wanted to be a lawyer. By budgeting his time and seeking the aid of others, he went to law school. He passed the Bar and now has a successful law practice.

His time outside the lung is limited. He uses that time to attend to his court cases and see to his other needs. At any time, he could have easily said *"I can't"* do that. Instead, he found a means of doing it. His mindset and perseverance are admirable. He used his mind to overcome his limitations with the help of others. He never said "I can't" and he employed the help of others to overcome his weaknesses.

He practiced breathing outside the lung until he could go nearly an entire day outside the lung. His determination, faith, and belief in himself allowed him to achieve what others thought to be impossible; it's a good thing he didn't believe it was impossible.

People who are successful have not been handed success. While there are some proverbial cases of the silver spoon, such as people being born into wealth, they are not lucky. One of the greatest achievements of wealthy parents is to teach their children the work ethic and mindsets that will allow them to retain their wealth.

If people say, *"Look how lucky he or she was"* they are embracing a negative idea or mindset that you must get lucky in order to succeed. There is no luck involved in success because we must do the work to achieve our goals. If you think others are succeeding because they somehow were lucky, then you will be waiting for your lucky day and that day will never come.

We see cases all the time where wealthy children squander their family's wealth, losing most or even all of it. This is because they didn't earn it and were never taught what it takes to handle that money. Were they really lucky? Is being left a fortune to lose being lucky? If they don't have the proper mindset to retain it, or the appreciation of the effort it took to acquire it, their luck will run short.

Those of us who have risen from poverty to wealth recognize the hard work necessary to achieve success. When someone tells me I'm lucky, I just smile and move on. By thinking that successful people have gotten lucky, you limit your own thinking and end up waiting for your lucky day, believing that you must get lucky to become wealthy.

Luck has nothing to do with rising from poverty to wealth. It takes hard work, self growth and creating a mindset that is advantageous to achieving your goals of wealth and happiness.

We can see this for ourselves when we simply make the observations of those who have gotten lucky; for example, most lottery winners will squander their money because they don't take the time to learn how to handle it before spending it. In addition, they are unable to see their weaknesses. They fail to hire someone to teach them to handle, retain and manage their money properly.

This is also true for those who come into money through other means such as lawsuits, retirement bonuses, huge contracts, and so on. Because they have internal beliefs that are not advantageous to keeping the money or using it to make more money, it's usually squandered.

In any case, if they didn't earn it, there is a high probability they will lose it. In the end, most lottery winners end up right back where they were before winning the lottery. As I've said, many times, this is mainly due to their inability to handle the money that was just given to them -- they didn't take the time or put in the effort in to learn how to handle it. They didn't pay the price, change their mindset or hire someone to counterbalance their weaknesses; it is the ability to produce money that allows you to retain money. If the lottery winner doesn't have this mentality, then it's likely that keeping their lottery winnings, making their life one of wealth and happiness won't happen.

By creating a successful mindset, doing the hard work, and learning how to achieve your goals, you remove luck from the equation of your own success. In many cases, if lottery winners, or those who inherit large fortunes, would simply hire advisors and coaches, they would be able to retain and grow that wealth. Keep this in mind the next time you have the thought *"Wow, that person is lucky!"*

The entire idea that it takes luck is negative because it marginalizes the efforts that were needed to obtain those goals. Negative people who bring negative thoughts into our lives, such as, *"it takes luck to amass a fortune or find happiness"* are not helping us. If we surround ourselves with unsupportive and negative people, we will find that our own thoughts become negative ones. In many cases, these people do not intend to hold you back; it's just that their mindset is bleeding over into your life.

A very common internal belief is that by finding faults in an idea we are somehow protecting the other person. This is so common that it's hard to recognize the negativity brought on by it. You must use your clear thinking skills to evaluate these types of thoughts and advice.

There is a great saying that goes something like this: *"Great minds discuss ideas. Average minds discuss events. Small minds discuss people."* By recognizing this in others, we can begin to easily see the quality of the people that surround us. Great and successful people are constantly talking about ideas that will inspire themselves and others to achieve more. Those ideas, in turn, lead to more success in their lives.

Meanwhile, average people are talking about material things like possessions or what they want. Small minded people are spending their time finding drama and faults in both their lives and other people's lives. Of these three types of people, try to find those who are inspired to do more with their lives in a real way; these people will be talking about ideas, making plans, and surrounding themselves with others who both teach and learn new ideas.

Shield yourself from negativity every chance you get. Negativity is like wearing a lead belt while trying to swim. People who bring negativity into your life don't necessarily do so in order to hold you back, although this is usually the end result. Unknowingly, they are putting their own fears onto you and your mindset. Through their own fears and apprehensions, they are creating within you that nasty "*I can't*" thought. In doing so, they are indirectly causing you to doubt in your own abilities; they are embracing the small or average mindsets.

The **five people** you surround yourself with the most will make up the majority of your own thoughts and attitudes. I cannot stress this point enough. Practicing this concept has greatly improved my life. If you surround yourself with five drama queens, you will likely become a drama queen since your outside influences are that of finding drama in everything. You inadvertently end up with a drama-filled mindset instead of a positive mindset of success.

If you, on the other hand, surround yourself with successful people who have achieved their goals and naturally support you in yours, then you will have a successful mindset. Since these types of people believe in themselves, you will end up believing in yourself and they will believe in you too.

When I started to surround myself with people who had a successful mindset, they never once diminished my ideas. They were, and still are, honest with their advice on how I can achieve my goals rather than criticizing them. The change in my own attitude was instant and it will be in yours also. I was amazed at how quickly the change took place and how their influences in my life were almost always positive and encouraging.

When a successful person doesn't know the answer, they can usually help you find someone who does -- they know what they don't know. They will also be quick to tell you they don't know something and refer you to someone who does. This level of honesty is empowering and helps build more positive mindsets in you and those around you. By knowing what you don't know, you will be able to find the counsel you need instead of worthless advice based on opinions or feelings.

Negativity comes in many forms and we must work to recognize it; sometimes it disguises itself in the form of concern for your wellbeing. In many cases, this is true for both internal and external negativity.

We live in a society that embraces excuses. People will give hugs and tell us that our failure is someone else's fault. This is never the case. While someone can create an obstacle, failure is your choice and yours alone. Remember that a setback is just that, a setback. Failure is a choice.

If this sounds impossible to you, and you believe others control your destiny that only means you are still working on your mindset. Once you know this to be true, then you will be able to move past any obstacle in your way. By accepting our setbacks as our own fault we can learn from them and move forward.

We see this acceptance of excuses and negative support all the time. Mary and John can't find jobs, people will try to support them by embracing their ideas that it's someone else's fault that they can't find a job, or that there are none available. Maybe they are supported in the idea that they are disenfranchised, and therefore, can't find a job; worse yet that there are no jobs, so they can't find one.

Whatever the case may be, Mary's and John's ideas of failure are being reinforced by others who are embracing all the excuses that allow them to give up looking for a job in the first place.

If Mary and John were my friends, I would ask them a few questions and offer true support in either finding jobs or creating the means of making money. I would not support their idea that there are no jobs or that they are somehow not at fault for being unable to find one. When we coddle someone's belief in their own failures, we only exacerbate the problem because we are embracing the *"I can't"* mindset.

Many people feel they are being helpful and supportive when they support someone else's failure by embracing their excuses. In reality, this confirmation of someone's reasons for failure only reinforces the negative thoughts that are causing the problems in the first place.

If you have been one of these people who constantly feels others are at fault for your own inabilities to succeed, then try changing your mindset. Try to realize that you are in control of your own thoughts and therefore your own life. All successes and failures begin in your own mind. Your mind rules your universe, so use it wisely. Remove those who coddle your negative beliefs that others are at fault for your failures. Start moving towards new goals and find those who will truly support those goals.

Another aspect of dispelling negativity is your own ability to change your mindset and have a Positive Mental Attitude (or PMA). Your PMA is important in your own ability to believe in yourself and to have faith in your abilities, in turn allowing the universe to answer your demands of life. Believing that you are worthy of success is key to being successful. You cannot do this without first having a PMA.

I have said this before because it's applicable in many instances of your mindset try to remember that, to be successful, you must first believe you're worthy of success. While this may sound easy, truly changing your mindset might be a bit challenging. Regardless, it is key to going past all of the challenges that you will face. You will have difficulty mastering control of the horses of your mind without first having a PMA.

Your PMA is determined by you and no one else. Like anything else you do to start controlling your mind, your PMA is a key factor in not allowing negativity to flow into your thought processes. To have a good PMA, we should try to recognize any negativity in both our own heads and from outside sources.

I used to think I had a positive attitude, when in reality I was embracing negative fears; developing a truly positive mental attitude requires not only embracing, but facing both fears and negativity, and then overcoming them.

I used to be an introvert, and I can tell you the fears that cause introverted thoughts and actions are negative in nature. Being an introvert can be harmful in your plans to achieve your goals.

To achieve great goals, we need to have others helping us, so being an introvert can prevent us from reaching out to others when we need to. We need to be willing to meet supportive people and interact with them in an honest way.

I found, in time, that my introverted nature was mainly caused by those around me. I had the wrong associations and those associations were affecting me negatively. Since I didn't realize this, I was becoming more and more introverted.

When I was introverted, I had a very hard time trusting people; I surely never took anyone at their word. I didn't possess the skills to evaluate people the way I needed to. Now, I seek out only those who practice the same type of life's philosophies that I do. There are fewer people doing this, but the people I do surround myself with are quality people.

I now enjoy being around the new people in my life. After all, I wasn't introverted by nature; I was simply unable to entirely relate to the people around me and drew into myself rather than seeking the right kind of people to surround myself with.

By following the philosophies, I have found a way of spotting likeminded people. Also, many very successful people either unintentionally, or intentionally, follow these philosophies. I highly recommend you start finding other teachings that support these ideas, not just this book and philosophy; in doing so you will more easily recognize people who are following one form of this philosophy or another.

The more you absorb from other teachers in the philosophies of success, the more you will start to recognize those who are using the philosophy. By finding others who have harnessed their three horses, you will be able to find quality people who are either successful or will be.

They may use different words, see things from unique angles, but their mindsets are ones of success. By practicing these philosophies, I was able to start recognizing quality people for the first time in my life. By coming up with Your Three Horses, I created an easy way to both apply the mindset of success and recognize those who have it.

I began to see the Three Horses in everyone who had achieved anything of significance. I was able to talk to them because our interests were the same. Even when the interests were different, we still had much to talk about. Our thought patterns and mindsets meshed up and a positive conversation became a natural thing. I began to realize that these types of people supported anyone on their journey.

My fears as an introvert were more about letting people into my life that brought negativity with them. I never realized this until I fully embraced the philosophy and put it into regular practice. Once I started to surround myself with likeminded positive people, again I realized that I wasn't an introvert at all. I actually had a different mindset than most people.

This doesn't make me better than anyone, just different than many of those around me. I had a different mindset and only needed to find my niche. Once I found that niche, things were off and running and I began enjoying life like never before. I worked for months and months without making a dime. I was striving towards goals and had the support of my wife & new friends.

I realized that I needed to plant the seed and let it grow. To be successful, we must start first with our mindset as the foundation of all success and happiness, and then grow our plans from there. Having a PMA is definitely part of that foundation we build to find success and happiness.

I was eventually able to get my own family on board too. My Positive Mental Attitude was becoming contagious. The better my attitude was, the better those around me felt about what I was trying to achieve; having a PMA is nothing to be taken lightly. It's the key to meeting quality people who will both support and elevate you honestly and correctly. It's also a key in dispelling the negativity in your life that's holding you back.

Do you surround yourself with the right kind of people?

Do you have a Positive Mental Attitude?

By having a PMA, you will be more confident. Additionally, you will want to surround yourself with as many people as you can who have a good PMA. By doing this, you will find that any previous negative feelings about the world, your own life, situation, and so on, will diminish to the point where you have none.

If you develop a good PMA, you will find that when you have a negative attitude about something you will recognize it almost as fast as it appears. Your ability to move past a negative attitude will become easier and easier as you maintain your own PMA.

If we first learn to recognize our own negativity, we can then see it better in others. It's rather amazing how easy it becomes with a little practice to simply move past a negative thought. Nobody can actually see inside anyone's head and know their actual thoughts. It is the outward projections of words and body language that can tell you all that you need to know about someone.

This also applies to you. Others will see you for who you are, whether you want them to or not. Sometimes people can get away with the deception for a short period of time, but eventually their true nature will show through.

I have a policy that I live by: Do not dwell on yesterday's problems or embrace the negativity brought on by them. Just move on, because what happened yesterday is over. Just let go of it, it's done -- you can't change it. If you hold onto any negative from yesterday, you are dulling your abilities today. We will later cover this more in the fear and worry section.

Emotional Control

CONTROLLING YOUR EMOTIONS & HARNESSING YOUR PASSIONS

Few realize the effect our own emotional states have on our lives. When using our mind to change our life, we must try to rebuild our entire life around our positive emotions. However, this philosophy only works when we have control of our emotions.

Controlling our emotions isn't always easy, but with practice it is obtainable. There are both beneficial and damaging emotions which we will have to deal with. Like everything in life, there are multiple sides to our emotions.

Our emotions play a large role in our overall outlook on life and, most importantly, our PMA. I recommend taking inventory of your emotions regularly and learning to control both the positive and negative emotions.

Abuse of emotions can play a role in the failure to achieve our goals. In some cases, they are a complete distraction from the goals we are trying to achieve. By using our emotions inappropriately, we can find ourselves in bad situations that are not advantageous to success.

I have taken inventory of my emotions and how they affected my life. Now, I not only take inventory of my emotions, I also take inventory of other people's emotions. One of the greatest indicators of emotional control is the ability to be both loyal and honest without a lot of selfish considerations. Loyalty breeds trust, another positive emotion.

Both loyalty and trust require honesty. Emotions -- like greed and selfishness -- are destructive when a person is attempting to show they are loyal, honest and trustworthy.

Having a poor emotional state weakens us mentally; it drags down our fortitude, making us feel powerless or weak. Many people who are unable to elevate their own lives are being held down at an emotional level. At the same time, they are dragging themselves down with a negative internal mental image of themselves.

Are there people who are holding you down emotionally or bringing negativity into your life? The people we surround ourselves with have an emotional effect on us. When you surround yourself with negative people it will have an effect on your own emotional state. It is important to both your emotional stability and your PMA to be able to recognize when someone else is affecting your outlook on life.

If you want to examine the level of negative emotions being sent your way by outside forces, just turn a TV on. Instead of watching a TV, pick up an inspirational book or put an audiobook on that will teach you a new way of thinking or reinforce a better way of thinking.

If you're reading this book, then you're on the right path. The reason you are not where you want to be is because you are not thinking the way you need to in order to find success and happiness. Your ability to succeed requires you to be positive. Keeping positive thoughts and having control of your emotions is another key in finding success and happiness.

The first, and most abused, positive emotion that is turned into a negative one is the sex emotion. The sexual desires we have are not just hormonal, they are an emotion also. By feeding the physical side, we can end up abusing that emotion. Nearly everyone likes physical sex, and the reasons for wanting it will vary from person to person and gender to gender. This emotion is known to be driven by a primal desire to procreate and fulfill an emotional need. However, if we look at nature, it is only humans that abuse the emotion regularly for self-gratification. Men and women both use the sex emotion to control and engage in conquest. If we weaponize sex in this manner we will drive quality people away from us. The use of sex as a weapon is the ultimate abuse of this emotion.

If we combine the sex emotion with love, we have a powerful mix of motivational emotions. This is most prevalent when a relationship is new and in its early stages. Many people enjoy this cocktail of hormones and emotions so much that when the initial emotions start to fade, the relationship starts to fade. As the relationship matures and develops into new emotions, they often give up on the relationship.

Failure to see the positive growth in a relationship by embracing the loss of the initial physical emotional and hormonal cocktail can, and does, lead people to end their relationships.

This happens because one, or both, of those involved don't realize that the initial high was caused by raw emotions and hormones. I believe it's this selfish desire to have the initial emotional and hormonal high of a new relationship never end that causes some people to have early relationship problems. This then becomes the cause of many relationship failures.

This type of relationship failure often occurs in young people who have not experienced it before. People can misinterpret the emotional and hormonal cocktail for love and when it fades, they now believe there is no love in the relationship. For young people this is a learning experience. However, when it continues to happen over and over again, it becomes a failure to recognize the difference between the initial highs and what love actually is.

People allow the absence of the initial emotional high to drive their decision making. We should see the benefits in the growth of the relationship, and take advantage of them and what's been gained, rather than embrace the negative side and see the loss. When we decide to end a relationship based purely on the loss of the initial emotions, we are making an emotional-based decision. Refer back to making decisions using the clear thinking model -- don't make decisions based solely on your emotional state. Let them clear first before making a decision about the situation.

The sex emotion can also lead to some seriously negative and immoral acts. These can include, but are not limited to: cheating, perversion, lying, deception and even sexual abuse of others.

However, if you transmute your sexual emotions into positive actions, you will find that being highly-sexed does not necessarily mean you are out conquering the world with your sexual desires. Many people who are very popular have a strong sexual presence, one that is naturally under their control. You can have a positive sexual presence without pursuing physical sex.

I have transmuted my sexual desires for my wife into a complete loyalty and dedication to her. My desire to please her isn't mainly physical. I support her in every way I can so she can reach her goals, and will do anything to see her happy. Anyone can use this emotion in bettering their own relationships by having this type of dedication and loyalty.

The level of honesty, loyalty and dedication to one another is enhanced by having control of the sex emotions and combining it with the emotions of love.

I don't speak lightly of this; trusting someone and being trustworthy in a relationship is first shown by control of your sexual desires and emotions. Many people do not realize the power of this emotion, especially when combined with love. The drive one can achieve by having control of their emotions, not just love and sex, is very powerful. Anyone is capable of this control once they recognize the power that is contained in their emotions.

When you embrace the positive emotions and forego the negative ones, you end up with a power that is both internal and projected out to others; it becomes fuel for your mind. Passion is the power of your emotions combined with your desires and can also fuel your persistence.

Negative emotions are a major source of failure. If you embrace greed, hate, intolerance, revenge, disdain, anger or any number of negative emotions, you will find yourself being seen as untrustworthy, and sometimes, vindictive. No one wants to be around people who are constantly gossiping about others or plotting to undermine people. These negative emotions rob you of your ability to move forward in a positive way. They can also lead to the creation of isolation and self-loathing.

There is one sure way of never being rich, and that is to hate rich people. That's all you have to do. If you have disdain for those who have more than you, then you will be unable to achieve what they have. The reason for this is simple. If you have negative feelings and thoughts about people who have what you want, you will never get it. After all, you won't want to hate yourself or see yourself as the things you despise in others.

If you hate wealthy and successful people, you will never be successful yourself. You simply don't want to be those things you hate. Therefore, your mind will ensure that you are never amongst them. We hear constant negative things about wealthy people, and we don't want to be those negative things ourselves. By embracing the negative ideas of others about successful people, you accept it yourself and become intolerant and hateful towards success.

The next time you see someone who has more than you, be grateful they have achieved those goals. Don't be jealous or envious, be genuinely happy for them. In this way, when you have those things, you can have them guilt free and graciously. Only by embracing this concept can you believe you will be happy, should you reach your goals. If you can't do this, you are putting a roadblock in the way of your own success.

In today's society, there are many falsehoods presented about wealthy people. One is that, generally speaking, they are greedy and selfish. Having wealth will only amplify those who you already are. Just like any other class of people, there are good and bad people. Passing blanket judgments means you are a bigot. Bigotry creates blind hate and disdain, and these are emotions you don't need in your life.

My experience with wealthy and successful people has been wonderful. I have found that successful people are usually kind and willing to do whatever they can to help you (provided you have the proper mindset, which they will recognize). Like anyone else with a successful mindset, they don't want to waste their time, or be swamped with negativity from outside sources. Time is their most valuable resource and they generally don't engage in any practice or associations that waste it.

As mentioned, positive feelings about those who have achieved what you hope to achieve are necessary. Those who have done what you're trying to do can provide counsel to you in a positive way. They usually don't partake in giving or receiving advice because advice is based on opinion, not facts. If you have negative feelings about successful people, you won't be able to have beneficial relationships with them.

Your emotional state is worn on your sleeve, whether you realize it or not. The more you are in tune with this philosophy the easier it is to recognize those around you who have negative thoughts and feelings. Your body language will give you away, just as the way you speak will expose you. You needn't be an expert in any of this, just simply start practicing the philosophy and you will start seeing these things in others. Once you do this it will become apparent how foolish it is to try and be something you're not.

By starting to control your emotions, first by recognizing them, you will start to improve your life. If there is one thing all of us can do better it is learning to control our emotions. We do this by using Clear Thinking and Self Evaluation. By examining ourselves we can start to recognize how and when to control our emotions. We will also recognize those who don't, or can't, control theirs and therefore we will be able to give them a wide birth, keeping that negativity out of our lives.

Good Character

KNOWING YOU "HAVE IT" & ACTING ACCORDINGLY

Many of the great teachers of this philosophy of success value quality people over all other things. People who not only resist temptations of poor character, but deny them entirely, are of the highest quality. Being of the highest integrity and character is important for both your own wellbeing and the wellbeing of those around you.

Mastering your mind and becoming a truly quality person is critical to success and happiness. The burden of guilt that is fostered by being of low character will affect your entire life. Do not accept anything less from yourself or others except that of being of the highest character.

I have developed a list of character traits I want to see both in myself and in others. We cannot demand of others what we are not willing to do ourselves, yet one of the hardest things to do is to point a critical finger at ourselves. In order to become of the highest character, we must continually point that finger in our own direction and examine what it is we are or are not doing.

THE TRAITS SEEN IN A QUALITY PERSON:

- **Honesty**
- **Integrity**
- **Loyalty**
- **Keeps their Word**
- **Goes the Extra Mile**
- **Spends More Time Listening Than Speaking**
- **Does Not Make Excuses**

- **Speaks Well and Concisely**
- **Doesn't Give Unwanted Opinions**
- **Admits They Don't Know Something**
- **Doesn't Challenge Another Person's Ethics**

Let's go over these one at a time. They are important in perfecting the Rider (yourself).

Honesty: Honesty is the foundation of all the ethical issues most people have. Being honest leads to everything else when seeking to improve your character or find people of quality character. If you're not honest, you will never have integrity. Therefore, honesty is the foundation for being a better person. Lies, deceptions, and omissions leave a wound inside you, like a dark hole that we try to fill or patch up with more negative actions. Because of this, the wound grows and creates levels of negativity that are very difficult to overcome.

If you are honest it will show, and you will also be able to recognize dishonesty in others. Without honesty, you will have little integrity. When you are honest, you create a level of trust that is the root of your integrity.

Integrity: When we talk about integrity, we are talking about being of upstanding quality in both your own actions and how you interact with other people. Having integrity leads to trustworthiness. Integrity means that your ethics can't be bought, and that you will do the right thing even if it is harmful to yourself. Many people lack this characteristic. They can be bought or sold far too easily.

Having your own integrity extends to what you expect others to do for you. Don't expect someone to show you something you are not willing to give yourself. You cannot ask people to do dishonest things without being viewed as dishonest yourself, nor can you have a lack of integrity and expect those you associate with to have it.

If you want to attract people of the highest quality, you will have to act with integrity. Integrity is a personal characteristic that leads directly to loyalty. In my opinion, integrity is one of the greatest traits a person can possess. By being an honest person of the highest integrity, you will have no choice but to show loyalty to others and expect loyalty in return.

Loyalty: This is a trait that I have found through observation to be lacking in many of us. When your only loyalty is to yourself, you will not attract quality people. When you are disloyal and ask others to be disloyal, you will not be an attractive person and people will shy away from you. Showing loyalty is key in having loyal people around you.

Your loyalty will be reflected in many ways. You will keep private things private, and you will do as you say to benefit the other person. You will do your best to never let your actions cause harm to anyone, especially those you claim a loyalty to.

Loyalty to others is a beautiful thing that breeds positive feelings and emotions. You will not only feel good about it, but people will also have more trust in you. When you are loyal, you will elevate yourself in the eyes of those you are loyal to, as well as others around you. When you are loyal, you will expect those around you to show be loyal. The value of this characteristic cannot be understated.

Being loyal is an attractive trait. Everyone wants to associate with loyal people that they can confide in or work with. There is no exception. Loyalty of others is gained by first being loyal to others yourself.

Keeps their Word: Keeping your word can mean making a phone call when you say you will to being a foster parent for a friend's child. Keeping your word leads to being viewed as having integrity, loyalty and being trustworthy. When you give your word, do everything you can to keep it.

If you can't keep your word, be the first to inform the other person that you can't keep your word. I also suggest you go one step further and lay out the reasons you cannot keep your word. Don't make simple excuses like, *"Oh, I forgot."* Unless, of course, this is the truth -- then you should be extremely apologetic. Expanding your reasons for being unable to keep your word is important. If you honestly forgot, *was there a reason? Why did you forget?* Don't just leave it at, *"I forgot."*

Don't tell someone you will definitely do something if you're not 100% sure you can. Be honest in your intent but ensure you temper it with the truth. If you say you will do something, try your best to ensure it gets done. If you're not sure, say "I will try" and tell the person why before you are expected to be there or have the project done. Don't wait until the next day or week later to explain.

One of the key aspects of keeping your word is to do your best to keep everyone informed. I'm not saying we have to be perfect and won't forget things once and a while, but how you handle the situation is important in how people will view your character.

One of my coaching students had some real issues with keeping his word... he had a major problem showing up on time. He'd say he would be there on time, but was always five minutes late. I informed him that if he wasn't five minutes early, he was late. I also informed him that by saying he would be there, then arriving late, he was showing me that he wasn't very trustworthy because he couldn't keep a simple appointment.

When I told him that 10 minutes early is on time, 5 minutes early is late, and that right on time was unacceptable, he took me seriously when he realized that I had rarely been late for an appointment; with the exception of one time, and had called him the minute I knew I was running late. The very next appointment, he was only a few minutes early. Instantly he said that he was late and I replied, *"Well, you're barely on time."* He said that his intention was to be at least 10 minutes early, but he had been hung up in traffic. I looked at him and said, *"That is exactly why you need to try to be here 10 minutes ahead of time."*

He also didn't like the idea that his trustworthiness would be questioned over such a simple thing, but it would be. Keeping your word on simple things will get you into the mindset of keeping your word on the bigger things. Mental habits are important. Make sure you develop good ones.

People are forgiving on this topic because we all have times when we are late, can't get something done or simply forget something minor. The point is, if you are doing this habitually, it wears down those around you and they become frustrated with the continual issues. This is when your character starts to come into question, and you will begin to be viewed as unreliable.

Goes the Extra Mile: The importance of going the extra mile can't be understated either. By going the extra mile and doing what you don't get paid for, you can express many of your positive emotions and traits, both to others and yourself.

People who don't go the extra mile can never demand anything more from life, since they don't give anything more to life. *How can you demand more money if you're getting paid for exactly what you're doing?* If you never give more than what is expected, then you are getting exactly what you're worth.

The characteristic of going the extra mile extends to all aspects of your personality; it will be viewed by others as a positive trait. If it isn't, you simply have the wrong associations. Going the extra mile will also help you identify those around you who have outstanding character.

Those around you who recognize your efforts and appreciate them are the types of people you want to be around, but this isn't to extend to those who would abuse your generosity. It should be viewed by others as a debt they owe you, not an expectation that you should provide.

To do more than is expected of you, with no request for compensation, is a quality that will carry you very far; those who do this are usually held in high regard. Those who don't and expect an immediate return for every little thing usually have short relationships with others. For those who do go the extra mile, we feel we owe them on the balance sheet of our relationship; when the time comes, we repay that effort if we can.

I have met many people whom I would go out of my way for and when the time came, *they were never there for me.* This is one of the most important things I look for in finding quality people to surround myself with -- if they don't go the extra mile in return, my opinion on their character changes to one of caution.

We should accept that this is a character flaw in this particular person, and just simply move past it. If we focus on these types of character flaws, we can draw negativity to us. We can create feelings such as disappointment or regret, which do not make the situation better. Simply accepting their behavior and learning from it prevents any future issues that could arise from our associations with that person.

In one instance, I was helping someone move. I made three or four trips to their new house, loading their stuff and unloading it into my truck. Several months later, I was moving, I told them about it and informed them of my schedule; they didn't show up until the last minute. Granted, I was moving further away, but they didn't offer to make one round trip or even come over to help load some of our belongings until the final day. On the final day, they did show up, but seemed more concerned about the stuff we were giving away rather than helping. In the future, I will show up to help them move if needed, but this will be done with less enthusiasm than before. I can't let their lack of character affect mine.

There were others, however, who offered up their help without being asked; they made several hour-long drives to our new house and did so with a smile. I will not only be there for their next move, but will go the extra mile to ensure that I'm there and can lend a hand in any way I can.

Spends More Time Listening Than Speaking:
Listening, rather than talking, is a trait that I admire. Early in my own life I was not good at this. I always had an opinion and was more than happy to share it, but today, my attitude is much different. I listen first and only speak of things I actually know something about.

Listening is a skill that is used to learn and show respect. Learning when not to speak or interrupt people is a key trait in showing respect.

By learning the skill of being a good listener, you can gain the respect of others. After all, we all like it when others listen to us. I have learned it's best to listen first, agree accordingly, occasionally cite examples that are personal, but spend the rest of the time listening. I call this mindset "learning mode". If you can start to put your mind into a listening (learning) mode, you will always be learning something when you are spending more time listening than talking.

Let's take this concept a step further and call this **learning on the next level**. By being around experienced people, hiring coaches and having mentors, you can turn simple listening into learning on the next level.

We can learn who people really are by *just by* listening. We learn who they are in regards to their character; we also learn about what is going on in their lives professionally. In many cases, you will get more information about someone on a more personal level than you actually need or want.

The ability to listen will provide you with endless amounts of useful information and knowledge. Listening to people with real experience can help you grow, learn on the next level. If you're constantly talking, you can't learn anything.

Does not Make Excuses: When you find someone who is constantly making excuses for why they can't achieve their own goals, or blames others for their failures, you should avoid them. When it comes to letting someone into your mind, try to recognize quality people with all the discussed positive thought patterns.

People who make excuses embrace your excuses and will not give you an honest assessment of your actions. When you have someone in your life that is embracing excuses, they usually are not honest with themselves either; therefore, they are not going to be honest with you. Remember that it's very difficult to point a finger at yourself and see your own shortcomings.

Many people who make excuses want to find others who will also embrace their excuses and validate their reasoning. This type of person tends to not only validate their own excuses, but also seek out others with perceived problems similar to their own to validate that person's excuse.

A perfect example of this is just about in any workplace. When jobs are hard, people tend to complain. This complaining is usually in the form of making an excuse as to why they are unhappy. They blame the job or situation for their unhappiness and they seek out others to validate their feelings. In reality, most people are not unhappy because they have a bad job -- they are unhappy because they made bad life choices which led them to a job they don't like.

I have done this myself; no one is immune. Until I decided that I was going to make a change in my life, I was stuck in a life that I didn't enjoy. By changing my mindset and having a plan of success, it only took a few months before I was out of that situation and on a new path, the very same path that has led to this book and the philosophy I now teach. You can do the same thing by evaluating your own character first. We shouldn't expect others to be something we, ourselves, are not.

When you have people around you who embrace excuses, rather than taking action to change the situation or move past the setback, these people become a negative influence on those around them. Most people don't even realize they do this, and because so many other people validate their excuses they just continue endlessly making excuses. People who don't make excuses tend to not accept your excuses. Therefore, they help you get past your problems by making you face the problem rather than accept a failure.

Speaks Well and Concisely: Seek out people who speak well and have a good mastery of proper language usage. This doesn't mean they have to have the most extensive vocabularies, it simply means they take some pride in what they say and how they say it.

Overuse of expletives is a sure sign of a limited thought process; cursing is generally uncalled for, and usually unacceptable. I cringe when I hear people cursing in front of others, especially when there are children around -- children are sponges and pick those words up quickly.

When you find someone who speaks consistently well in the face of the negative chatter around them, you will usually find that they have respect for themselves. I, myself, had an extremely bad habit of cursing after my time in the military -- expletives seemed to be the main adjectives used in the military. Therefore, expletives became mine too, even when I was no longer in the military.

It took me years to break the habit of expressing emotions through expletives. I still occasionally slip, but now recognize it immediately and apologize (whether needed or not) for my slips.

Nonetheless, I have a decent vocabulary and will use it without thinking about it. Over the years I've extended my vocabulary because of the books I read and the people I surround myself with. Also, it doesn't hurt to mention that my father was a semantics and English teacher.

Doesn't Give Unwanted Opinions: Someone who constantly has an opinion usually doesn't know what they are talking about. In my experience, the most vocal and opinionated people generally shouldn't have an opinion in the first place.

When you find a person who constantly pontificates how much they know, is a sure sign to be cautious around them. People like this generally want you to take their advice and do what they believe (not *know*) is right.

Opinions are pretty easy to spot and are usually based on emotion rather than facts or experience. Yet another source of opinions is hearsay, which means you have no facts and you're just going on what someone else has told you. Still another sure sign that you are hearing an opinion is the emotions that the person attaches to it, no matter the source of their belief. They may say things like *"I feel you should"* or *"I hate it when"* or *"I know better"* with no actual reasoning behind it. These are sure signs you're about to receive a useless opinion.

On the other hand, you may hear things like *"I don't know, let me find out "or "In my experience"*. Mindful opinions can also come in the form of poignant questions, such as *"How did you come to that conclusion?"* Or *"Where did you find that?"* Those who find counsel and give counsel rarely have a baseless opinion.

Admits they Don't Know Something: Opinions, as mentioned, are not facts. People who know what they don't know are always ready to admit it. This character trait is hard to find. When you find someone with it, you are almost guaranteed to find someone of high quality.

There is no shame in not knowing something. Only small minds that are based in opinion see flaws in those who admit that they don't know something. I'm not saying that over my lifetime I didn't give out a lot of worthless opinions, but I did see value in asking questions and doing a lot of research to form a valid opinion.

I now try to never give an opinion unless I have all the facts. If I do, I always state this is just my opinion and that I really don't know. This type of conversation usually comes up when talking with people who insist on talking about other people or topics that they know nothing about.

Often as a life coach, I find myself in the situation of listening to the opinions and stories of people I know nothing about. I routinely make it very clear that *"I don't know"* and that *"It's not for me to decide. I wasn't there"*. With almost all coaching students, initially there are times when their focus is purely on excuses and what other people have done to them.

They usually have many opinions about things and in order to be a coach, I must listen. In doing so, I'm not usually listening to the story per se. What I'm doing is evaluating the story to find the roots of the issue; I'm learning before I form an opinion. When I do make a decision, my ideas about the situation are not based on assumptions -- they are now based on the available facts, as perceived by the student.

My goal is to get them to change their mindset, not what the story is or how they came to their conclusions. In these situations, I try to get to the point of knowing what I previously didn't know. It's done by listening and evaluating the situation so that I can help them change their mindset.

Doesn't Challenge Another Person's Ethics: Lastly, in seeking quality people, you need to be aware of people who want you to breach your own ethics. These people may ask you to take something you shouldn't or give something that you shouldn't sacrifice. They may ask you what your opinion is about another person because they are seeking to verify their own opinions.

People of low quality are constantly seeking validation for their excuses and opinions. These are the same people that will try to draw you into conversations involving other people. If you have ethics and integrity, you realize that this is a violation of your own ethics.

When people intentionally, or even unintentionally, ask you to engage in violating your ethics, they are not going to be a benefit in your life. Hold fast to your ethics and be aware of those who ask you to violate them.

A good example is a recent situation I found myself in: There was a person who wanted me to give them the class materials from my expensive classes. I wasn't comfortable in doing this, and told them that. They continued to push for the materials. Eventually, they figured out I wasn't going to give them the materials, and I never heard from that person again. This shows how easily you can remove that type of influence from your life.

The Law of Attraction is constantly at play; it never rests and always delivers you exactly what you are asking for. Ensure that you are what you are seeking in others. I guarantee you will eventually find it. If things seem dark and difficult, and there are few people of character in your life, look to your persistence…have faith and trust because you will find quality people, especially if you are a person of quality character.

The perseverance you display in your search for people of character, as well as your own growth to improve your character will deliver quality people to you which will make you a quality person. People of character will want to be around you, because you are a person of quality character also.

In closing, not only should you seek quality people, but you should first do your best to become one of these people. By changing yourself to meet higher criteria of personality and character, you will attract those who are of that same character.

"Be the type of person you would like to meet."

- Greg S. Reid

Excuses and Alibis

STOP FEELING COMFORTABLE WITH FAILURE

Embracing excuses is a common cause of overall failure in life. If you want someone to coddle you, tell you why and how you're a victim, there will be a long line of people out there ready to help you.

People who embrace excuses will see personal challenges, societal failings, and other people's faults as a reason for their own failures; in turn they will accept your excuses. They will support these ideas, and accordingly, help you accept that your own failures are out of your control.

Your persistence is a key factor in seeing past everyday challenges. Believe it or not, there are many people who have gone through what you have and have still succeeded. There are many who remained on top while having the same problems you are facing. The reason for this is simple: They didn't believe a struggle or setback could stop them.

These people didn't accept the excuse or make alibis for their setbacks. They just moved on and kept growing from each challenge. They were gaining from the process that provides setbacks as a learning tool. These people refused to accept the idea that any obstacle could stop them.

Those who overcome obstacles are not waving a magic wand in the air and asserting that obstacles don't affect them. Instead, they continually send out their desires and passions to everything and everyone around them and refuse to allow an event or person to stop them.

Many people have even lost the functionality of their bodies and gone on to make incredible, inspirational contributions to humanity. In turn, they make themselves successful in the process.

Helen Keller couldn't see, speak, or hear. She went on to become one of the best educated women of her time. She even eventually learned to speak and presented speeches about her journey.

Steven Hawking lost all use of his body and ability to speak. He went on to become one of the greatest scientific minds of our time.

Christopher Reeve was the star actor in Superman during the 80s. After an accident, he became paralyzed, but this didn't stop him. He went on to be elected Chairman of the American Paralysis Association and Vice Chairman of the National Organization on Disability. Reeve co-founded the Reeve-Irvine Research Center, which is now one of the leading spinal cord research centers in the world. He also created the Christopher Reeve Foundation. The same fortitude and persistence he used to become an acclaimed actor was used to continue his success, in spite of his disability. He didn't allow his disability to define him; rather, he defined his disability and used it to achieve even greater success.

The list of successful people who have faced tremendous challenges goes on and on. The difference between them, and many others, is one of acceptance. They don't accept excuses or failure. These people simply refused to be told they couldn't do something, nor did they listen to anyone who told them they couldn't add value to their lives.

It's also important to note here that they embraced a flexibility to change direction. When the circumstances in their lives changed, they rotated and took a new direction in life. Instead of embracing self-pity, they moved on, taking their challenges head on and pushing forward.

When you see your challenges as being the end, they then become the end. When you see them as setbacks or obstacles to be overcome, then they will be overcome. The mindset of winners in life is that of never accepting defeat. I have said this before, but here it is again. A setback is just that, a setback. Failure is a choice.

After reviewing each of my own failures, I found a common trend. I had stopped trying and embraced an excuse for giving up. I gave up and let the idea go. I didn't put the necessary desires and passion to use or practice the persistence necessary to reach my goal and move past the setback.

By embracing excuses, you destroy persistence. Without persistence, passion and desire fade into oblivion and we are left with nothing, not even faith or trust. The simple act of accepting failure brings your entire mind to a halt and you come to a stop. This isn't to say you can't bring persistence back into your control -- you absolutely can; pick up the reigns and gather your thoughts back in by using persistence. If you do, desire and passion will return to you. We can always continue a halted journey by simply dismissing our excuse, learning from the event, finding the positives, and then finally moving forward again.

I say failure is a choice because we choose to walk away and let go of our dreams and desires. Excuses are poison to your dreams and goals. However, people embrace them regularly and are very comfortable in doing so. We make them up and do our best to find them and those who will validate them for us.

As mentioned, if we want to find people who support our excuses we can. You could even say there are certain support groups that exist to support your excuses; hundreds and even thousands of people will support you in your excuses to aid you in your own failures. Until we give up on the idea of accepting an excuse, we will be handicapped by them.

I find it bewildering that some actually believe they are helping when they embrace another person's excuses. They believe this type empathy is helpful, when in reality it isn't. If we do this, either for ourselves or others, we not only embrace another person's excuses, we also give ourselves room to have those same excuses.

Making excuses is easy to do, which is why so many embrace an excuse rather than solve the problem. We can blame someone for our failures or we can learn from them and move on. We can blame a situation or circumstance because it's easier than solving the problem and moving past it. No matter how you view it, you are responsible for your acceptance of an excuse and therefore for your own failures.

No matter how bad the situation, you don't have to accept it because it will only be used as an excuse for future failures. Too often, people dwell on past events in their lives and fail to recognize them for what they are -- setbacks and challenges are only events in our lives, nothing more. We can choose to grow and become stronger from them, to make them motivational points in our lives, or we can embrace them as excuses for our own failures.

Failure is always a *choice*, no matter what has happened to you. While we may need to take time to rethink and change our goals or find a new purpose, ultimately, failure is up to us. It's up to you to make the final decision on whether or not those events empower or destroy your goals and dreams. If someone has wronged you, for whatever reason, allowing that to destroy your dreams just gives that event more power than it should have ever had.

If you rely on your Persistence and go back through an event that seems insurmountable, you can overcome it and you can learn from it. You can find the positive in it, but it all depends on your attitude and belief about the event. Our minds are so powerful that they can demand anything of the universe. If we use the powers of our mind to overcome obstacles, they will be overcome.

The power of your thoughts is your greatest gift. It gives you the ability to think your way out of everything and manifest whatever it is you want. In turn, we also have the power to think our way into or out of anything, good or bad.

Thoughts become things. Nothing was ever created that wasn't first envisioned in the mind. If you envision an event as causing your own failures, it's sure to be manifested. Your failure will be the result of your own beliefs and willingness to give up and accept the excuse.

If you believe you are oppressed, then you will find oppression around you. If you believe that people are holding you back, then the universe will send you people who will give you the opportunity to believe you are being held back. It's purely about what you truly believe and what actions you are willing to take to overcome obstacles or avoid them in the first place.

When we put it into our minds that something is going to stop, or hold us back, the only possible result is being held back. If we can realize the power of our persistence and our abilities to overcome challenges, nothing can stop us. The same powers of the mind that are used to cause failure and embrace excuses can also be used to create success.

Excuses only have as much power as you give them. Straightening things out in your mind, not accepting things that we see as holding us back, is a great first step towards achieving success. Don't hold your failures in high regard; instead, see the lessons learned from them. This will help them fade into the background and become points of strength. They will eventually emerge as lessons learned and events you overcame.

With every lesson we learn, we are more skilled at moving forward. We can therefore move forward with more confidence. Dwelling on failure can cause us to lose confidence, motivation and find excuses to continue to fail.

Never facing a challenge almost always ensures we will never have the confidence to meet those same types of challenges in the future. When we learn from them and truly believe that we are stronger from them, they can become great sources of confidence and strength.

During one real estate deal early in my investing life, I had found a house I was sure I could get financing on. I did this on another person's word. I don't believe there was any ill intent on their part. This deal, however, was going to blow up in my face and create one of the darkest moments of my new life.

In a meeting, I was told I would get the house at a certain price. I was left with the impression that if I did this, he would finance it. I did just that, I went back to the sellers and negotiated the price. But when I brought the deal back, he told me to go find the financing. Well, I was under the impression that because I got the price he wanted, he was going to help me find the financing or finance it himself.

Since I was under the impression that I would get help financing, I made the deal in a way that I normally wouldn't. I told the owners that I should have no problem getting financing -- this was my mistake. I wasn't in possession of all the facts, and I hadn't asked the important questions to see if he was going to finance the deal himself or not. I made the classic mistake of assuming he would, rather than asking if he would. How could there be any malice on his part? I was the one that failed to ask the questions I needed to. I had made the blunder that I teach others not to. I had assumed I knew something that I didn't know.

I usually inform people that I will try my best, but that there are no guarantees. This time, I was confident that I already had financing one way or the other because of my meeting with the other investor.

When I went back to him again, he informed me that he didn't have the money and made a few suggestions as to who to go to to find the money. I contacted those people, and they drug along for a couple of weeks, leading me on. In the meantime, I was leading on the owners of the property who were in a bad situation and needed out. Again, I didn't place blame on the potential lenders, they had no idea what was going on. It was I alone who put myself in this situation.

In the end, the deal fell through and I was responsible for putting these people, who were already in a bad situation, into a worse situation. While I could have blamed others and used it as an excuse because they didn't come through, ultimately, it was my fault. I'm the one who implied I could do the deal. I'm the one who didn't come through. I'm the one who didn't ask the right questions. I still feel bad about this deal to this day. It was a dark spot in my early investment career.

The sellers dissolved the contract with me. I mutually agreed and sent them back their original documentation. I included an apology letter and a small check as a gift and show of gratitude for their patience and time.

I was protected legally as the contract expired harmlessly and we dissolved it in the meantime, but it wasn't my wellbeing I was concerned about. I was concerned for the stress my inability to come through on the deal would cause the sellers. Good intentions are worthless if you approach them the wrong way. I received a well-deserved chewing out, and continued to look for financing in the meantime, all to no avail. In the end I had put forth the effort, but my implication to them that I could find financing was wrong.

I vowed to never let it happen again. I wasn't going to put my character on the line by not doing my own homework or making assumptions. I was guilt-ridden about it and had a large empty dark spot in my chest, a void that seemed to run deep. I had no intentions of putting these people into a worse situation and there was no way my success was going to be at the expense of others. While I had made an error, it could be overcome. I however had to first accept that I was the one who made the error.

I made the decision that I wasn't ever going to put someone in a bad position again. Remember my requirements in being a quality person? I also must live up to those same requirements. I had to develop a new policy for myself and how I was going to do business. As many negative events in our lives could stop us or slow us down, I decided to make this one a policy changer. Since I felt an extreme sense of guilt over this event and failed deal, I decided that the cost of trying to make deals like this work wasn't worth the gains.

From that day forward, I refused to enter into any contract I didn't already have the money to do. Also, I would not sign a contract unless I'd made it extremely clear that I didn't have the money and had no idea where I'm going to get it. If the seller makes the slightest implication that this is unacceptable, then there would be no contract signed.

I didn't intend to mislead the seller on this deal, but did whether I intended to or not. I must take responsibility for that, otherwise I'm using excuses and not solving the problems.

I refuse to allow any excuses to cover my errors; nor will I allow anything else cloud the fact that I made a bad decision. Those events are my fault and no one else's. I must put my own ethics and character above all else, and my new policy would ensure that this type of situation would never happen again.

I must take full responsibility for what happened. Even though there was nothing I could do to stop the outcome, that isn't an excuse for what happened. The only way to correct an error like this is to ensure it never happens again, and you must learn from it to do that. I pride myself on being honest, upfront, and truthful. Therefore, I would have to learn from this event to ensure it wouldn't happen again.

To give in, though, and allow this setback stop me would also be giving up and using this event as an excuse. The acceptance of self-responsibility, and your unwillingness to accept any excuses, both helps you develop new plans and prevents you from embracing excuses for your own failings.

Therefore, there was only one choice: Keep moving forward with a new wisdom and a <u>new policy</u> in place to prevent that type of thing from ever happening again. After all, there are no excuses that are acceptable for failure.

While there was nothing illegal or unethical about not being able to obtain financing, that wasn't the point. There was a moral obligation to both them and myself, of which I failed to deliver on. My new policy would ensure that this type of situation doesn't happen again.

Are you making Policies to Improve Yourself?

Do you accept responsibility when it could easily be placed on others?

Like everything else in this philosophy, it's best to do some self-evaluation when facing setbacks. Look back over your life and evaluate the times you have given up and accepted failure; it will always be accompanied by an excuse for doing so. Eliminating the excuse in your own mind will allow you to realize that failure was a choice, it was your choice.

Causing your own setbacks isn't a bad thing, it's inevitable and it is simply a learning process. Without doing this (I have done this dozens of times now) we don't learn the lessons we need to gain wisdom. It's my hope that the lessons presented in this book help you to avoid having to go through some of the setbacks I have had to go through. Or, if you hit a spot like I did in my failed real estate deal, you can develop a new policy to prevent it from happening again and grow your own character. If you start now, you can change your life. Of that, I have no doubt.

The entire purpose for this book is to help a fellow traveler on the road get past the obstacles they are going to face. At the same time, my hope is this book may enrich your thoughts and widen your perspectives. However, this still relies on your own abilities to improve yourself. If you lack faith and trust in yourself, then letting go of excuses is even harder.

Have faith in yourself, don't embrace excuses.

Conquering Fear

BEATING FEAR, & FINDING FREEDOM

Fear, worry, and anxiety are all means by which we can easily choose to fail and not achieve our dreams or find success. In order to eliminate them, we should try to understand them. The following chapter is the means by which we can understand the most crippling fears and worries we have. We will then try to combat them together. We can use our abilities of observation to determine what we see as the fears, worries and anxieties that cripple us.

All of us, no matter how strong we may seem, have fears that will drive our decision-making. Understanding the difference between a beneficial fear and an inhibiting fear is necessary in knowing which fears are holding us back.

THERE ARE 3 PRIMARY TYPES OF FEAR:

- **Instinctual**

- **Instilled**

- **Imaginary**

Instinctual Fear: This is the type of fear that protects our physical body from the realities of nature. This first type of fear, like all other types of fear, is in our own control. We can embrace these fears or we can ignore them. In either case, we are in control.

A perfect example is the instinctual fear of death that protects us from danger. In the face of death or attack, it kicks in and we will act accordingly. The fight or flight response is triggered and we either avoid danger or face it head on.

Instilled Fear: This is the kind of fear that's placed upon us by others, or learned because of some experience we have had. These are the types of fears we learn to have.

We can learn or accept fears that are taught to us by other people. Learned fears also fall into this category because when we learn a fear, we instill it into our minds.

Events such as burning our fingers on a stove could lead us to end up fearing fire. This type of fear isn't always negative. It should, in most cases, be expressed in the form of respect rather than fear.

Imaginary: These are the fears that our imagination dreams up. They're the most insidious type of fear because often, you are afraid of something that hasn't happened or can't happen.

When imaginary fear is combined with instinctual and/or instilled fears, it can become so debilitating to us that it leads to our own demise; there is no worse fear than imaginary fears we've dreamt up. There's nothing more destructive or menacing to one's own being than the fears they imagine themselves.

Imaginary fears lead to anxiety, worry, and a slew of other emotional problems that society is continually plagued with. One commonly imagined fear we have is that of illness.

For a short period in my life I worked at a hospital and saw more people worried about being sick and their own health than people who were happy with their health and living their lives. There was a constant stream of regular visitors to the hospital who had very little wrong with them. Regardless, they found many reasons to make an appointment to be seen and checked to ensure they weren't ill.

Constantly focusing on illness, either directly or indirectly, can lead someone to being ill. Hypochondria, or the imagining of illness, is a medically diagnosed problem some people have. They so deeply believe they are sick that they manifest the symptoms of the illness in which they believe they have. While there may be nothing actually wrong with them, their suffering is real to them.

When we make an examination of these three basic causes of fear, we can see how these fears affect our ability to do just about everything in our lives. There is a constant barrage of misleading information that is being used to make you afraid of something that you should not be afraid of. This fear eventually destroys your ability to think logically; until you make a concerted effort to think clearly and find the facts, you are simply living in fear. Once you are living in fear, you are an ignorant tool of those who wish to control you.

We can find these types of fears being used to market products when we hear radio advertisements or watch television commercials. Fears are pushed on us to sell products such as cosmetics, pharmaceuticals, insurance, and a long list of other products.

Cosmetics use the fear of criticism in the form of non-acceptance.

Pharmaceuticals use the fear of illness or lack of wellbeing.

Insurers use the fear of loss.

These instilled fears are used to control our spending habits. The subject is extremely complicated because many of these products and services are needed. In some cases, natural fears or instinctual fears are combined with instilled fears to create an opinion in the viewer's/listener's mind that is more advantageous to purchasing their products. I'm not saying their goals are deceitful or unethical, I'm saying you need to be aware of what you are hearing and use clear thinking to make decisions about the topic.

Fear is used in many forms to affect how you think and believe. Fear of anything prevents you from attempting to obtain or attempting to do that thing which you are afraid of.

This subtle control over your mind is so easy to do that it's done daily, hundreds of times. You are exposed to thousands of advertisements every day. Between cell phones, the internet, TV, and radio, there is a constant barrage of fears being sent your way. Instilling fear into your mind is an excellent way to sell you products and take from you your own self-worth. They do this by showing you what they want you to believe you should be or look like. In doing this you feel belittled and want to live up to the unrealistic standards being projected towards you. The cure for this uncomfortable feeling is usually the product that's for sale.

Manipulators are also very good at using fear to sway your opinions. They instill fears into you or amplify ones you already have to cause you to draw into yourself and disbelieve what others try to tell you. The more you fear something, the more susceptible you are to this type of control. People who manipulate you can only do so if you remain ignorant of what their actions are doing. Some are so good at it that you must take serious time evaluating what it is they are actually doing. Once you become practiced in this, you will start to recognize it more easily, allowing you to avoid it entirely.

Fears can be the root of most worry and anxiety. If we have some unreasonable fear about other people's opinions of us or what could happen in life, this can cause us to be over-cautious. While being cautious is a good thing, having too much caution will inhibit our ability to move forward in life.

In most cases, however, fear is based in ignorance because we do not have all the facts and information we need. Because we are not in possession of all the facts, if we accept advice as gospel, other people can easily instill fears into us and manipulate our opinions. If you don't know something, you simply don't know. That does not mean you should be afraid of it.

While instinctual fear makes sense, imaginary and instilled fears do not always make sense. It is usually a lack of knowledge, or the embracing of ignorance, that allows others to instill fears upon everyone around them. While they may be genuinely concerned for your wellbeing, it is their own fears that are creating the concerns in the first place.

When I went into real estate investing, I received very poor advice from people with no experience in it about how dangerous and ill-advised it was. Fortunately, I did not embrace their fears because they were not based in reality. I say this for one reason: none of the people who were giving me real estate advice actually owned any real estate outside of their own homes.

If I would have listened to their fears, I could've easily become afraid of my own actions. I, however, had already spent a couple of years studying the concepts of investing in real estate. In addition, I was also expanding upon the philosophies of success and developing my own philosophy.

Recently I saw a video that was forwarded to me. It was of a young woman who was convinced it was dangerous to go outside. She was so afraid of running into men who were going to assault her that she didn't want to leave her home. She admitted that she had never been seriously assaulted, but considered someone looking at her to be sexual assault. This type of absurdity boarders on a mental disorder, but I will guarantee this is an instilled and imaginary fear that this poor woman needs help with.

She was convinced that all men were looking at her with sexual intent. She was convinced that every time someone looked at her it was in a critical way and she was being judged for how she looked. These are all imagined fears that now cripple her life. While this case is a bit extreme, it does prove my point: You can be manipulated by fears you shouldn't have and those fears can be instilled into you when you allow your imagination to solidify them.

One of the major things that I learned in studying the philosophies of success was that fear is one of the main components to failure. When you fear something, it is likely you will not do it. If you do it and there is fear, it's likely you will fail. The reason for this is quite simple: you will seek out the reasons to fail because you are focused on your fears and not your success. This focusing on fear creates unneeded worry and anxiety, and to relieve ourselves of all these negative feelings, we generally choose not to act.

Focusing on fear, in any form, is a great way to destroy your own confidence and sabotage your own efforts. I don't say this lightly. Fear is the main cause of worry and anxiety. Once you start to embrace fear, you will start to have more fear, worry and anxiety regarding everything in your life. The train doesn't stop there; if you continue to embrace those fears they just keep growing and growing.

If you want to move past fear, there are several simple steps you can start to take right now. The first is to recognize what type of fear you are having. *Is it instinctual fear? An imaginary fear? An instilled fear? Or, is it a combination of fears?*

If someone says something to you that creates some form of anxiety or fear, it's best that you do some research before you make the decision to embrace those fears. When you research those views, ensure that you are looking at both sides. Find the reasons to be concerned, while at the same time, learning how to elevate those concerns by learning the reasons not to fear that decision or situation.

Sometimes, this research can be quite lengthy because in many cases, people make decisions based on fantasies and imagination. The people telling you these things may not have the knowledge, or the dedication to find the knowledge to alleviate their own fears, and instead instill those fears into you to validate their own.

Almost all worry is based on ignorance or lack of knowledge. The same is true for many of the fears that impede our progress in life. You cannot make a clear decision or embrace clear thinking if you are not in possession of the facts and willing to accept those facts.

I want to stress that people tend to ignore facts in favor of their own beliefs and/or emotions. I would also like to point out, again, that opinions are usually not based on facts. Opinions create advice. Facts and experience create counsel. Many people do not understand the simple distinction between the two and how helpful counsel is in comparison to useless advice or opinion. Instead they end up embracing the fear, worry, and anxiety that comes with this lack of understanding and knowledge.

The first step to alleviating fear is to ensure that you're in possession of all the facts before you embrace a fear or make the decision to believe something you are being told. Being in possession of all the facts will allow you to make sound decisions rather than reckless decisions based on your emotions and opinions.

I don't remember where I heard the following story, but it is a perfect example of how all this works. We can look at this situation to make clear what it means to be in possession of the facts.

A business owner is approached by a stranger at his office one morning. The stranger tells him that his employees are breaking the law. Unaware of this, a sudden anxiety comes over the business owner.

The stranger goes on to tell the business owner that he will ruin his business by taking this information public, unless of course, he is paid to keep the information under wraps. The business owner, now in a panic over being blackmailed, asks the stranger to return the next day to be paid. After thinking it through, he decides to call the police to inform them of the attempted blackmail.

He knows deep down that he hasn't done anything wrong and that if there are employees breaking the law, he can fire them to save his own credibility. He has taken the first step in clear thinking and eliminated the fear of being blackmailed. The police inform him that the man is a con artist and has done this to several other businesses. He makes arrangements to have the police there when the man returns the next day. The man is arrested and the business owner goes on doing business, unhindered by the burden of his worries about the incident.

By using clear thinking, he has eliminated his fear and has found out the facts. In this case the facts were simple. The man accusing him of a crime was actually a criminal and a con artist; without these facts the business owner may have embraced his fears and given into the threat, even though the threat was baseless.

The three types of fear are fairly easy to understand. However, while most people will say they understand, it's difficult to truly understand the effects of these fears until we take the time to examine our own thinking on the subject. On an almost daily basis now, I see those who are constantly embracing their fears and creating worry in their lives or allowing others to create fear, worry and anxiety for them. In many cases, they justify their fears based on the opinions of others who shouldn't have an opinion on it in the first place.

There are seven primary fears that ruin our attempts to succeed in life. They are rooted in instinctual fear but are exacerbated by both imaginary and instilled fears. When we look at the basis of fear being that of instinctual, instilled, and imaginary, we can also understand the seven primary fears. This is done simply by recognizing our thoughts that revolve around these concepts.

The following seven fears are the primary fears that stop most people from advancing in life. See if you have any, or all, of them affecting you.

THE FEAR OF:

- **Poverty**

- **Criticism**

- **Ill health**

- **Loss of love**

- **Old age**

- **Death**

- **Loss**

While some of these fears may seem instinctual, if you really examine them, you will find that the basis is truly imaginary or instilled. Let's explore each of them in a little more detail.

Fear of poverty: This is simply the fear of not having enough. The more you worry about not having enough, the less you will have. A simple fact found in the philosophies of success is that you attract what it is you think about the most. If you think of poverty constantly, then you will be impoverished.

The fear of criticism: The fear of criticism is purely imaginary. This fear is imaginary because you are putting your beliefs into your perception of what others are thinking, even if they are not thinking in that way. The fear of criticism is easily conquered with self confidence and the ability to simply do the things that you want to do.

All you need to do is not care about what others think. I know we've all heard this cliché before, but we must use it because it's very true. To quote Dale Carnegie: *"One of the surest ways to overcome fear is to keep doing the things we fear."*

I used to have a fear of public speaking, writing for others, and expressing my own views through writing and teaching. This was not because I didn't believe my own views, but because I put my fears into the heads of those around me, imagining what they were thinking. What I didn't realize was that it didn't matter what they were thinking. What mattered was what I was thinking.

The fear of ill health: If we worry about ill health, we can become ill. We can fear ill health so much that we actually create our own ill health. We can create ulcers, nervous problems, and many other conditions simply by focusing on ill health.

The fear of ill health is exacerbated by outside sources that take the imaginary fear of ill health and increase it with instilled fear. The combination of imaginary and instilled fear creates a truly dangerous combination when it comes to your health.

The fear of the loss of love: This is a twofold fear. It involves both the death of loved ones or the loss of someone we love in our lives. The more we fear this, the more worry and anxiety we create in our lives.

I have seen instances where the fear of losing a relationship partner has actually driven that partner away. This is more common than it needs to be. This fear creates all kinds of other emotional problems too, such as worry, dread, and jealousy.

The fear of old age: This fear may seem instinctual but it's not; it is purely imaginary. If you believe that you will be decrepit in your old age, then it's likely you will be decrepit in your old age. There is no reason to waste time or mental energy worrying about this. You are going to get old, so why worry about it?

The more you worry about becoming old, losing your physical and mental abilities, the more likely you are to lose them. Again, it's the imagery you send out to the universe that comes back to you.

I have seen people who are in their 50s who look like they are in their 70s. When you talk to these people, you will usually find there is some underlining reason. Sometimes it is based on excessive worry or a constant focus of getting older.

In other cases, we see people who look to be in their 40s and they are actually in their 50s. When you talk to these people, they make jokes about getting older but rarely embrace their age. They are mentally young at heart and their physical bodies show this belief.

The fear of death: This is simply the fear of the unknown. If you fear death, as most people do, you can spend your life worrying about the inevitable end. We know we're going to die, *so why fear it?* If we fear losing loved ones, it's inevitable that we will lose them, so there is no reason for fear of it. Death will happen to all of us, including our loved ones.

We need to come to terms with it because of its inevitability. If we fear losing loved ones and focus on that, we are worrying today about something that will happen in the future, something that worry isn't going to change. At some point, everyone you love is going to die. *Why fear the loss today?*

It's very empowering to not fear your own death or the death of others; this is a power many people do not enjoy. Once you stop fearing death, then you can truly enjoy life and make the most of its abundance.

The Fear of Loss: I believe this seventh fear is as powerful as the fear of death. The fear of loss can be crippling to both financial and personal advancement. Too many people fear losing what they have so much that they end up causing more losses for themselves.

Fearing the loss of what you have creates the need to search for security, but security is created by continual advancement, not worry. If we fear losing our jobs we will likely never try to advance beyond where we are at. This fear stops us from taking any risks or chances at all. If you want to advance you must take advantage of opportunities as they arise. If you don't then you are embracing the fear of losing what you have.

There are constant opportunities to eliminate the fear of loss, but many of us don't even realize we have this fear in the first place. We seek security; even when there is none, and we embrace our fears while falsely feel secure when doing it. By taking these simple concepts about fear and doing some self-evaluation as to what's causing our own fears, many of them are conquered rather quickly.

Realizing that imaginary fear is the cause of most worry and anxiety, we can also begin to conquer those negative thoughts in our lives. While there are rare cases where some situation has created a chemical response in the brain that causes an irrational fear, this is not the case for most fears.

The regular embracing of fear creates a negative field of energy around all of us and even around those you surround yourself with, meaning that your own fears can become a great influence on those around you. In turn, you should recognize the fears others have and how they influence your life. By recognizing them, you can easily eliminate them from your thought process.

There is little you can do to eliminate fear while you continually embrace fear. By embracing both rational and irrational fears, we create a state of mind that creates worry and anxiety. There's little you can do towards your own self-improvement if you choose to embrace fear, worry and anxiety.

One of the reasons that we learn to embrace all types of fear is that our instinctual and instilled fears are very useful to our survival, especially when growing up, as we are most susceptible to learning to embrace these fears. What that said, there is a difference between wisdom and fear. Simply being afraid of something doesn't mean you possess any wisdom on the topic.

When we're growing up, it's usually a painful experience to learn not to engage in certain types of behavior. Other wisdom is imparted upon us by our parents or other associates, as they give good counsel and share their wisdom with us.

Being afraid at the instinctual and logical level helps us to survive. When we take those thoughts and feelings and extend them to other actions, we can impede our own progress. We can begin to fear things we don't need to be afraid of.

Many of us know we need to make mental and psychological changes within ourselves to improve our lives. It's usually some form of fear of change that keeps us from doing the things we need to do and acting on that knowledge to make those improvements.

Our own irrational or imaginary fears prevent us, in some cases, from moving forward. When you evaluate your reason to fear a change, it's usually based in the unknown. When you don't know what's going to happen, and fear it, this is an irrational fear, a fear of the unknown. At the same time, it could bean instinctual, rational fear that helps us protect ourselves in situations that are physically threatening.

So, *what can we actually do about this?* The best way to combat this type of fear is to gain the knowledge that provides security in taking action.

For example, if you don't want to climb down into a dark hole in the ground because you don't know what's in the hole, this is a rational fear. Just jumping in the hole could be deadly, so the fear is rational. Anyone who did just jump in the hole would be viewed as an extreme risk taker.

There are ways we can alleviate those fears though. We can shine a light in the hole and see how deep it is, and then we can look around to see what's in the hole. We can, once we know what's in the hole, apply either wisdom or logic to the knowledge we have just gained.

Once we have the information, this fear can either be reinforced for good reason or abolished because there is nothing there to fear. You shouldn't embrace fear when you have the knowledge about what's in the hole. Wise decisions are made with no fear, as it's not required to make the decision.

All advancement in life is like looking into that dark hole, not knowing what's inside. To advance through life, you must gain the knowledge to know what's in the hole. We now know that it's wise to shine a light in the hole to see what's in there before we decide whether to jump inside or not.

Before we advance into the darkness of something new, we can use knowledge that will provide the light to allow us to travel into the dark with wisdom, rather than fear and apprehension.

When I told you my story of going from homeless to having a business, I then told you that I lost my tattoo studio. Here's why: everything came crashing down because I was harboring a fear that was based in ignorance. I had started the business and I honestly didn't know what I was doing. I feared what I didn't understand and neglected to take action because of that. I made the mistake of avoiding issues such as business licenses and other legal issues that could affect my business.

Instead of shining the light in the hole and gaining the knowledge of what I needed to do, I just embraced the fear and ignored the issue.

Eventually the inspectors showed up and shut me down. I hadn't done any of the necessary steps for having a legal business in that state. By allowing my ignorance and fears get the best of me, I lost what could have been a very successful business.

This, however, was a very valuable lesson in learning to play by the rules. I was later able to relate that to the irrational fears I had at the time. No matter who you are, you will have to play by the rules of the game. If you embrace a fear of those rules, it will catch up to you.

By understanding that fear is generally based on a lack of knowledge, we can apply this simple concept of gaining knowledge to alleviate fear and continue to move forward. If you desire to become a real estate investor, it is highly recommended that you study real estate investing before you jump into that dark hole of the unknown.

The greater the change you need or want to make in your life in your life, the more knowledge you will have to gain to alleviate all the fears that are associated with that change. Facts and knowledge remove the darkness and illuminate your path.

If you don't gain the proper knowledge, it would be like standing over that dark hole in the ground, peering into the dark without a flashlight. You are choosing not to gain any knowledge of what is in the hole. There may be a bag of gold lying in that hole, but if you choose to not shine a light in the hole, you're choosing to embrace fear rather than gaining the knowledge to overcome it. *A wise man shines a light in a dark hole before deciding his next move.*

The ability to embrace fear and take the easy path to safety is so tempting that it actually holds many of us back from ever achieving what it is we want to achieve. There are many reasons that people are not successful. Fear is only one of them, but it's a big one.

Fear, worry, and anxiety are some of the primary causes of people never taking a chance. This is because they haven't learned to mitigate risk by having knowledge. These emotions are also the cause of failing to take actions when you need to.

I love educated risk, I do not like gambling. An educated risk is when you try something new based on education by outside sources that have succeeded at what it is you would like to do. This form of counsel may come from books, mentors, and coaches, such as me.

When you mitigate your risk with knowledge, you reduce your fear, worry, and anxiety. The simple gaining of knowledge can empower you to take steps that you never believed you could.

So, shine a light in the hole and see what's in there before you before you decide to walk away. Know this: If there's a bag of gold in that dark hole, you will miss it unless you shine a light in there first.

Eliminating Worry

LEADS TO HAPPINESS AND SUCCESS

Worrying is treacherous, at best -- it drags you down and, in many cases, creates unwarranted fears and anxiety. Worry, anxiety and fear are intrinsically linked, as each works in causing the other.

One of the more interesting concepts we'll cover in this philosophy of success is the relationship of worry and anxiety to fear, and of fear to worry and anxiety. They all feed one another, and increase the negativity that comes from them.

Here is a calculation which illustrates this. You can use it to examine your own worries, anxieties and fears. Worry plus fear equals anxiety. W+F=A. Interestingly you can switch all of these around and end up with the same result (negative emotions). No matter what vantage point you view the calculation you will find that eliminating two parts eliminates the last.

For instance: F+W=A or A+W=F. As you can see, no matter how you flip this simple calculation around, the end result is the embracing of fear in one form or another. Worry, anxiety, and fear are all intertwined; one does not exist without the other.

The outcome, in every calculation, will contain fear. If you're worried, you fear something. If you have anxiety, you fear something. Anxiety and worry lead to fear. An exception is in the case of false anxiety, which we will cover shortly.

This is an inescapable circle in which only your process of thinking can get you out of. While all three are intrinsically linked, we can eliminate each one of them one step at a time. To eliminate worry and anxiety from your life, you will have to manage your fears. To reduce your fears, you will have to manage your worry and anxiety.

All of these are the primarily negative emotions that lead us to failure and stagnation. Remember the hole: You need only a flashlight or source of light to see what's in it. The same goes for your advancement in life and reduction in your own fears. In many cases, you are only lacking in knowledge.

Many people are in a constant state of worry. As mentioned, worry is a side effect of fear. Fear can be a side effect of worry. Worry creates fears no sooner than you start to worry. Since both are intertwined, we should find a way to eliminate both of them from our daily thought process. Without fear and worry there is no anxiety.

Anxiety is usually the end result of worry and fear. It can also be the cause of worry and fear when the anxiety is unfounded. One way I learned to deal with anxiety was to start recognizing what I call "false anxiety".

When we start to recognize that many of our anxieties are simply a self-induced false anxiety, we can start to eliminate that false anxiety from our lives. I say they are self induced because it is the acceptance of this anxiety that causes the problems. Again, we have control of this in some form or another, we need only exercise that control.

Almost everyone I've ever spoken to has had times where they are sitting in a chair, driving down the road, or talking to someone and they have an episode of anxiety. They don't know the cause of this anxiety, but the immediate results are almost always the same -- suppression of positive emotions replaced by an attempt to discover where the anxiety is coming from. This is usually followed by some form of fear and worry about the anxiety and the whole circle is set in motion.

When a false anxiety comes to us, we are immediately brought into a negative state of mind. This is because anxiety usually has a cause. It's almost always associated with some fear or worry. False anxiety (or anxiety with no cause) simply creates the emotional responses without any reasoning. While this false anxiety may have an origin, that origin event is not taking place now. So, the anxiety you are having isn't actually real, it's false, and this is why I call it false anxiety. While the anxiety is real, the cause of it isn't real, at that moment. Because of this, it is very advantageous to recognize a false anxiety. When you do, you can calm down and take steps using the clear thinking method to resolve the false anxiety.

This false anxiety should not be confused with your sixth sense. One of the reasons we need to learn how to manage fear, worry, and anxiety is so that we can more readily recognize our sixth sense when it speaks to us.

Before we can do this, though, we must learn to manage false anxiety. There are many reasons we may have false anxiety. For the purpose of this book, we are going to just brush the surface because this topic alone would take an entire book to examine and there would still be questions.

When a past event leads to future false anxiety, it too can be overcome. In my case, when I was in the service, I worked the flight deck as a final check technician on the catapults. One day I was signing with the pilot, preparing for the launch of his plane. He started signaling frantically for me to get down.

Since I was standing on the deck looking up at him, all my attention was on him and the plane. With all the jet noise you couldn't hear anything during flight operations. I immediately followed his instructions and jumped to the deck, laying down and covering my head instinctually. This was when I saw parts from something hitting the deck around me. When I stood up, there was a crashed helicopter only a short distance from me; its rotary blades were shattered all around the deck where I had just been standing.

Unbeknownst to me at the time, this event was going to create some deeper problems later in my life. I had escaped with only a couple of scratches on my elbows from diving to the deck. After my discharge, this event had a greater effect on me than I would have imagined.

I would sometimes have extreme anxiety if someone startled me from behind. I would almost go into a rage at the person who startled me. Later, I discovered that this experience had somehow engrained itself into my subconscious. I was having a false anxiety about things happening behind me that I was unaware of. To me this was unacceptable, but it took years for me to sort it out.

I took this event and turned it into one of my greatest advantages in combating false anxiety. When I would get startled, I'd calmly say to myself, *"It's the helicopter. That's all."* Eventually, it became a mental habit which alleviated almost all of my stress and anxiety when startled from behind. It now takes a lot to actually get my adrenaline going, whereas before I was always on the verge of a sudden rush of anxiety, adrenaline, and fear.

I used this to form the idea of controlling all false anxiety and started to apply this in my own life. You too can apply this tool. Here is what you can do: First, recognize the fact that your anxiety is false by simply asking yourself, *"What am I anxious about?"* Then, follow up by asking, *"Is this false anxiety?"* If so, *what can you associate with it?* Then say to yourself, *"It's just the helicopter."* *(Or whatever you believe it to be).* You can also just dismiss it by telling yourself *"This is just a false anxiety."*

Your anxiety could be stress brought on by work, a relationship, or another current or past event. Try to associate your false anxiety with something that will allow you to dismiss it. This takes a little practice, but once you form a mental habit of doing this, it will just start happening.

It's merely your version of the helicopter that creates a false anxiety. Useless anxiety can be beat by simply knowing what your helicopter is. If it's nothing extreme, then it should be fairly easy to dismiss once it's recognized as a false anxiety.

However, in most cases anxiety is actually based in subconscious fears or lack of actions taken to resolve it. I have also found that living under extremely stressful conditions can cause this type of false anxiety.

False anxiety leads to useless worry. Worry and anxiety lead to fear. **Whether the fear is founded or not, it is real, and it is negative.**

You may be surprised at how easy it becomes to start eliminating these useless false anxieties from your life if you apply clear thinking and action to resolving them. You can use this same technique to dismiss some forms of legitimate stress, also. Ask the same questions and instead of trying to relate it, ask yourself if there is anything you can do about it. Form a plan of action and take those steps to eliminate the anxiety.

This isn't to say it has to be taken care of that second. This way of thinking is a mistake many people make: They want the anxiety cured at that moment, when it can't be. Instead, form a plan of action, even if it stretches out over years, and stick to it. Then, each time this anxiety comes to you, you can answer it by saying to yourself, *"I'm doing everything in my plan. There is nothing more to do right now."* You will find that if you are sticking to your plan, then your dismissal of the anxiety is easily accepted. I continually hear people talk about what they are worried about. Inside, I smile when I hear people say things like this. It isn't because I'm enjoying their plight, it's because I realize that many of their problems are based on the fact that they are continually worrying about them. You do not have to be like this. By taking actions to resolve your worries, both internally in your thought process and externally to resolve them, you can eliminate them. Try to start to recognize useless, unwarranted fear and worry in those around you and in yourself, and eliminate those negative sources from your life.

I have found that it is extremely difficult to get many people to realize that worrying about their problems is usually useless. The moment you tell someone that they shouldn't worry about whatever it is that they're worrying about, they will immediately get defensive. They defend their negative mindset and reasons for worrying.

When this defense goes up, it is usually based on one's own pride and emotions. We don't want to be told what we should or shouldn't be worried about, nor do we like it when others tell us what to do. After all, we have a state of mind in today's society where worrying about everything is accepted, and not only is it accepted, it's expected.

An exercise I like to do when listening to others is hearing how many times they say *"I worry"*. Just recently, I was working with one of my contractors. We were having casual conversations. I noticed that he said he worried about something or another at least 10 times during the day. By paying attention to how many times somebody else says they worry, you may begin to realize how much you're worrying yourself. If you pay close attention to this, you will realize how much worry is imposed on you. We're constantly listening to other people's worries. As I listen, I'm careful to ensure that their reasons for worrying do not become mine.

You can indirectly, or even directly, worry more yourself because of other people who are constantly telling you of their worries. Until you have the mindset of not worrying and the understanding that worrying is useless, it's very easy to get caught up in this worrying game.

When you start evaluating the statement *"I worry"* and mentally begin to associate it with its causes, whether it's caused by fear or anxiety, you will begin to see that it is usually caused by both.

This avalanche of negative emotions and outlook causes us to project a desire into the universe to have everything we're worried about happen. The last thing any of us really want is to have everything we worry about delivered to us, yet this is what we do when we constantly engage in worrying.

The more you worry, the more worry will find you. If you are subconsciously seeking worry, the universe will deliver more of it to you; after all, you must want more since you keep thinking about it. This basic Law of Attraction can be proven to every individual on the planet, especially when it comes to worry, since most people engage in it constantly. If we simply do the self-evaluation to see how many times both our good and bad thoughts have actually been delivered to us by the Law of Attraction, we can validate it.

While the Law of Attraction can work wonders to your benefit, there is a truly negative side to it. This side is that worry seems to breed fear, and that breeds more worry and anxiety. You attract more of what it is you fear and worry about into your life. Simply letting go of your fears and worries can change what it is that you are attracting into your life.

I want to note this here because it is important: Your worries cannot affect other people. If you are worried about a loved one, or anything else that you might believe can affect another person, you can't bring that fear to them. In other words, your worry isn't anyone else's worry. The law of attraction will not bring negativity caused by your worry to another person because you are worried about them. This attraction of negativity due to your own worries will not attract that negativity to others.

However, if you *impose* your worries by bringing those concerns to that person, they may start to have the same worries. In this case you have indirectly helped bring those things to them by bringing your concerns to them. You may have just instilled a fear into the other person. The same goes for you, and this is why you can't let other people's concerns become yours.

Fortunately, we cannot project our worries onto somebody else because the rules do not allow you to do that. The rules are simple: You are in control of your own mind and no one else's. Therefore, others cannot put thoughts into it unless you allow them too.

If you're worried about what someone else is doing, it will have no effect on them unless they allow your ideas to create worries or fears in their minds. You can use this rule to keep other people's worries out of your head. We should be cautious when we bring our concerns to others, many of us don't realize how we can actually affect another person's reality.

The more of this negative energy that you surround yourself with and listen too, the more fear, anxiety, and worry you will end up having. This, of course, can be stopped by not accepting someone else's worries into your mind and not worrying in the first place.

We've all known the person who has an outstanding positive attitude. No matter what happens, they constantly maintain a smile and never seem to worry about anything. For many people, this becomes an annoyance. They want to see this person have worry and anxiety over the same things they do. This isn't intentional, but rather a need for validation.

When people like this refuse to accept worry or anxiety, annoyance grows in the negative people around them. What I recommend to you is to be the person who annoys the negative people with your positive outlook on life. You will empower your own mind and find freedom in less worry and anxiety. Your desires will be that of what you want and not what you are worried about.

Beating Worry

There are several ways in which you can learn to stop worrying. One way to stop worrying is to live in the day or in the moment. There is nothing you can do about what happened yesterday and tomorrow isn't here yet, so live in this one day, this one moment. Do the task at hand and focus on what it is you are doing. Make this day the best you possibly can. Make every action a success by doing it the best you can and applying yourself in that moment. Stack up the little wins and increase the positivity in your life.

You can also take actions that will alleviate your worry. Make moves to eliminate your worry by seeking the knowledge to eliminate it or developing a plan to address it, and then take the actions needed to resolve the issue. By sticking to your plan, you can easily tell yourself you are doing all you can do, and if you are doing all you can do then worrying is useless. Taking actions changes your focus from worrying to finding solutions and resolution. When you have a well-developed plan and take every action on schedule, when worry comes to you, you can easily dismiss it.

To worry about what happened yesterday is to create anxiety about something you cannot change. Yesterday is gone, and tomorrow has yet to come. Bear this in mind when you start worrying about the past or the future.

This isn't to say that you shouldn't make quality plans for the future; it's simply to say that you shouldn't worry about those plans. If you sit down and think about it, almost none of your plans go exactly as you planned them to go. Once you have a plan and are taking the required actions needed and making the adjustments as the circumstances present themselves, then you are doing all you can.

You can lay down plans for the future, but live in the moment, knowing that those plans are likely going to change just as quickly as you make them. This is why we want goals that are surrounded by a set of continual actions. Remember, one of the keys to success is to be flexible and recognize when changes to our plans need to be made.

Notice I say actions, not action. This is because it will require multiple actions of varying nature to reach any goal. You must be flexible in your plans and work towards your goals, but there is no reason to worry about them.

Let's say you have serious money issues; your electric is going to be shut off or your car is going to be repossessed. You must develop a strategy to deal with this. This is where most people fail: They engage in worry rather than making a plan. Eventually everything collapses and they still have no plan of action.

If these things are going to happen, we should try to figure out first why they are happening and find the root cause of the problem. This helps us decide which direction to move in. Let's say you lost your job and don't have enough money for the bills. Put together a plan to handle today's problem *today*. What can you do *today* to help resolve the problem? Find a way to make money? Decide what priorities are most important and focus on those? If you waste time worrying, then you are losing time in which you could be solving the problem.

When my wife and I both lost our jobs within months of each other we were in this very situation. We were going to lose our house and cars, and our credit was going to be shot. We had to make a plan of action.

We decided first that we needed the cars to generate money, and moved those to the top of the list. They were paid first. Then we would pay our basic bills, such as electric and water. We needed those to use our computers to keep searching for jobs and have light at night and water to drink.

When the unemployment started to run out we decided we would leave the house and move to a less costly area. We downgraded our living situation and rented a trailer. We had also realized that our credit was shot but we didn't need to worry about that right then. There was no need because there was nothing we could do about it.

We regrouped after moving and made more plans. We needed a way to generate money so I took a job that would get us by while we worked on our other plans. The top priority was to get my wife's career off the ground, and then we could work on mine. This was the long-term plan. We regularly developed steps to reach those goals; we took actions to better our living situation, and eventually did so.

Notice, we didn't spend time fighting about money, wallowing in self-pity or blaming others for our failures and current situation. All of that would have been a waste of time because it didn't resolve anything. We instead put a plan of action into place to change our situation and worked on it as a team. We were so busy working out our plan that we had little time to worry about the things we couldn't change.

We look back now with pride in our accomplishments and our resolve to find solutions to those problems. We did eventually get our creditors repaid and started to restore our credit. While we could have done some things better, it didn't matter because we did something. We took actions and stuck to them.

I don't speak of eliminating worry nonchalantly. I know it can be difficult. However, from my experience and through observations I've made in my life, combined with the studies I have engaged in, I can say this with confidence: **If you are stuck worrying, you can stop by taking actions and keeping busy on your plan.**

In hindsight, I also realized that we were so busy working our plan that we hadn't even thought about getting the TV turned back on. Once in a while we would put some old DVD's in the player, but other than that, we went months on end without ever watching the TV. We didn't have time to waste watching TV.

This is when I came up with the calculation of wasting time watching TV. If you watch 2 hours a day of TV, you are wasting 30.33 days a year that could be better spent taking actions towards reaching your goals or solving your problems. I also realized that by not watching TV we had eliminated multiple sources of negativity from our lives. We no longer paid attention to politics, sports or commercials; it was a freeing experience. Ever since then we have not had cable or satellite service, as to us it is just a waste of time and money.

Many people have worries about where the money to pay bills is going to come from. This is usually based on past experiences that are now over. No two days are exactly the same, even if they seem to be.

You need only take the actions that bring money to you, just as you have throughout the past when you have been successful at paying your bills. The actions you're taking today will provide for tomorrow so long as your plan today is to achieve that goal.

By separating yesterday and closing the door on the past, as well as by closing the door in front of you on the future, you can start to focus on the present and put your plan to work. Do today's tasks the best you can and tomorrow will be better. Try to constantly have small wins; in this way we make every day a winning day.

Another way to dispel worry is the same way we dispel fear. Simply gain knowledge about what it is you are worried about. Sometimes your worry is simply not being in possession of all the facts. Take some action to elevate your worry. Do the research to gain the knowledge as discussed in the clear thinking section.

In a case where a good friend was in financial trouble, I and others advised him to seek counsel from a lawyer. He was worried about losing his house and the current life he had. After seeing the lawyer, he was given a plan of action to get out of his circumstance and keep his home. Previous to having this knowledge, he was only guessing as to what the outcome might be.

After seeking counsel, he found he could work things out and retain the things most important to himself and his family, including his home. Worry was converted to hope and a plan was formed and acted upon. He told me a weight had been lifted and that he felt good for the first time in a long time about his situation.

Keeping very busy and focused on what you are doing doesn't give your mind time to think about the things you are worried about. If you are sitting at home all day doing nothing, you will find that worry likes to creep its way into your thoughts. An idle mind leads to a fearful and worrisome mind.

Keep busy with positive actions. I encourage the "Three Actions a Day Rule". I take no less than three actions a day towards my goals, and you can do the same. They needn't be huge actions or big steps. Little steps work great, but you should take them every day. Remember, all the little wins add up to bigger wins.

The second of the Three Actions a Day Rule is this: If you have spare time, find three more actions to take. Continue this until the day is over. Eventually all your little actions lead to big opportunities and solutions to the things that are causing you to worry. Many people don't like to stand idle, and I believe this is because the results of taking those little actions lead to big opportunities and fewer worries.

Your mind cannot think of two things at once. This, too, is fundamental to drastically reducing the worry in your life. If you don't believe me, try it. Try to think of the project you are working on, maybe reading this book. Now try to think about something else at the same time. The two thoughts cannot co-exist at the same time -- you are forced to choose one or the other. Choose the positive one that doesn't involve worry. By focusing on the task at hand and fulfilling your goals, you won't have time to worry.

Keep adding tasks to your life based on both today and your future goals. Send some e-mails, make some phone calls, or simply study to learn more about what it is you want to do. Find positive ways to fill your time and you will find ways to eliminate worry.

If you worry about money, the Three Actions a Day Plan can resolve it. Take three actions a day to earn or make the money needed; develop new plans to work around the issues you have. Don't waste time worrying about it. I believe you will find that the money you were worried about becomes easier to find when you stop worrying and have a plan of action to make more happen. Maybe even a book on earning side money or finding ways to make passive income would be a beneficial tool. You will never know unless you take action towards finding out how you can achieve the goals you have now set for yourself.

If you embrace the concept that you're going to learn from your setbacks and the challenges you face, then solve the problems that are presented by them, you will have no fear or worry. Everything that happens, whether it's good or bad, becomes beneficial in reaching your goals. Once you have this mindset you don't worry about setbacks or challenges, you simply work on solving them.

I enjoy solving the problems that arise from my setbacks; it's a challenge I look forward to overcoming. I'm not hoping for setbacks, I just don't fear or worry about them. After all, they can each be resolved -- all are an opportunity to learn and grow. You can do the same thing. Just change your mindset, if you haven't already, and believe that setbacks are part of the process and are also beneficial in the long run.

The main reason most of us constantly embrace worry are the pre-existing bad mental habits we already have. We get into these bad habits, and like any other habit, they can be hard to break. When you wake up, recite your major purpose and know that today will be a good day.

Find three things, first thing in the morning, that will help you reach your long-term goals and add them to a day planner. Start taking actions as soon as you wake up, don't give your mind time to wander off into a state of worry. A good attitude, and a small win first thing in the morning, can lay the foundations of a great day. If you do this every morning, you will find you are stringing great days one after the other. The winning becomes addictive, you want more of it. This positive outlook on the day, first thing in the morning, can help pull any adverse situation you face back into your control.

Sometimes that action is simply ensuring that you smile in a mirror and think about how grateful you are for everything you have, no matter how much or how little. Know that today is going to be a great day, regardless what happens during the day.

We can fill the empty moments, which could otherwise create day-long worries, by simply not thinking about them and creating a plan for that day.

Have everything you want to do in a day planner, especially when you first start practicing this. I use a notepad to write down the things I want to accomplish. Today I may have as many as five things for my major goals and 10 or more for my minor goals. Work on solving problems to the best of your abilities rather than worrying about them.

Try to practice the art of not worrying, it's a fine art that I know you can master. You will be amazed at how much better your Positive Mental Attitude and overall view of life becomes. Don't embrace fears, instead, dispel them and gain the knowledge to face them with wisdom.

Solve the problems; make informed decisions. Don't allow fear, worry and anxiety to rule your life. Rule your worry by not having it in the first place. This will empower your mind, and therefore, strengthen your entire outlook on life and achieving your goals.

New Thinking, New Results

FINDING THE KEYS TO SUCCESS

The Three Horse Philosophy is based on the imagery and the powers in and of your mind. It's my belief that the imagery we send into the universe is more powerful than the words we think in our heads or speak out loud. It's more clearly understood by all around us. We can project these images more easily when we think in terms of our Three Horses being individual aspects of our mind and self. Your Desires, Passion and Persistence are tangible aspects of your reality; they are your inner powers and will help you succeed.

When we imagine our desires and passions, and embrace our ability to persist, we send out a complete version of what we are trying to achieve. When I meet a new coaching student, I want to see them in person or through video conferencing. I want to know what they look like, so I have a complete picture in my mind of the person I'm trying to help.

In my mind, I picture them in the exact place they want to be. Even if initially I may not understand them, I follow my instincts and develop a plan to help. I do this first by listening to them, hearing their story and seeing where they are straying from their path. I can only help someone find their way back to their path if I know who I'm dealing with. One must have their own goals and desires to build upon. This image of the happy or successful coaching student allows me to envision them when we are done, having achieved exactly what it was we set out to achieve.

In most cases, I need to first start by working on the mindset of the student, no differently than I had to work on my own mindset. Thankfully, my mentor worked with me to smooth out the wrinkles, and now this is what I try to do for others.

To find the keys to your own mindset, self-evaluation is necessary. Yep, there it is again: Self-evaluation and meditation on who we think we are and how we can change to become someone new. If we don't change our mindset, we can't become someone new. If we don't become someone new, then we can't change where we are going or who we are in order to find more success in life.

When we want to achieve something new, we have to do something new. In most cases, I find that many people focus on things that slow them down or prevent them from moving forward at all.

Many people are worrying rather than living; they are focused on the worry rather than the solutions. Getting your focus off day-to-day drama and onto your own progress helps get things moving in the right direction. You can never harness the powers of your mind or use the rules of the universe to your benefit if you're focused on the wrong things.

I also see people thinking for other people, putting their thoughts into the heads of others. They imagine what it is someone else is thinking and believe it to be true, when they actually have no idea what that other person is thinking. I was guilty of this before my mentor and coach helped me through it. By over analyzing situations, I was making decisions for other people without knowing what they were actually thinking. I had it in my head what I thought the other person wanted, even though I really had no idea.

By recognizing the *"I don't know"* versus the *"I think I know"* I was able to start finding a new mindset. I learned not to make decisions based on what <u>I thought</u> was going on in another person's mind. This was only inhibiting my progress since I was always second-guessing other people. In reality, I didn't actually know what they really thought or felt about the situation.

When you stop thinking for others, you free up your mind. You can negotiate your situation based on your own needs and the actual facts you have. If you're getting into any kind of business, this mindset of knowing what you don't know is useful for negotiating. This also applies to jobs; don't assume to know what you think your boss thinks of you. Instead, be forward and ask questions that will answer your unknowns.

As a past manager, I had my ideas about employees. On more than one occasion, people asked for raises that were less than I was prepared to give. That's right, they asked for *less* than I was going to give them in the first place. In their heads, they were thinking for me. They were thinking about what I might be willing to give, rather than asking for what it was they wanted.

One instance of an employee asking for less was when it was annual review time (therefore, time for raises). I went over the review of his previous year and was ready to give him a $1/hour raise. This was the most my boss allowed me to give. I even had to prove why that person was worth the raise. When I finished his review, which was outstanding, I asked the usual question.

"What do you want to see in a raise?"

He thought for a moment and said, *"$0.50 an hour."*

"You should think more highly of yourself than that," I said.

The employees knew that they could get up to $1.00 an hour and that was what I was prepared to give in this case. I gave him the $1.00 anyway. He was an even better employee after that. I don't think it was the money though. He truly appreciated the fact that he was valued.

In another instance, when buying real estate, I was trying to make a deal for $40,000. However, the deal wasn't viable at that asking price. In a meeting with my mentor, he asked what would make the deal work. I told him $25,000 or less.

He looked at the numbers and said to bid $22,500, an underbid with patience. By patience he meant to not accept anything else, to walk away if it didn't work, and to wait to see if the deal came back. He said to stop thinking for them, as *"you don't know their situation even though the numbers you have support your offer"*. He added that they probably hadn't told me the whole story yet, but they would if they accepted the offer.

I approached them and made the offer of $22,500; I told them it was the best I could do. This price made the deal viable and profitable. They said they would think about it. A few days later they called and said that if I could cover roughly $2700 in additional costs, they would accept the $22,500 offer.

With that added, the deal was right where I needed it to be. I was thinking for them instead of making the offer that works and letting them decide. When I did so, and explained my offer, they accepted it with a small negotiation of the $2700 in past due bills. It was going to work out for both of us now.

My problem wasn't that we didn't know what was going to work; it was that I was making the decision for them while not actually knowing the situation or what they would say to the more realistic offer.

I actually didn't know what they were going to do. This was a valuable lesson for me and would serve me well in all my future deals. I may have known better, but it was my bad mental habit of putting my thoughts into what I believed others were thinking that initially would have led to a bad deal. It was a limiting thought and limiting thoughts do just that: they limit what you think you can do and what you can actually do.

The new mindset was the proper one. **We never know what we don't know.** When attempting to change our mindsets, one of the hardest parts is to realize the mental gymnastics we do as we form our thoughts and beliefs about what other people are thinking.

We tend to put ourselves into the other person's situation to try to make decisions for the other person without having the facts. If you do this, it's time to stop and recognize that you are not in a position to make decisions for others. It's more likely than not that you are not in possession of all the facts.

In many cases, friends and family will try to help you by playing devil's advocate when they don't actually know what's going on. You have heard the questions or concerns of others, we all have. You get questions like *"Are you sure you're making a good decision?"* Or statements like *"I don't think that will work."*

There is a long list of unintentionally negative support that's dealt out in the hope of helping you. In most cases, this support is generated by a mindset of creating security and fear of losing security. People put themselves into your mind and give advice accordingly. Since they don't know themselves, they assume you don't know either. They would be afraid so they assume you should be afraid also.

If someone is trying to influence your decision, politely find a way out. One of my favorite ways to deal with that type of thing is to respond something like this: *"Well, I hadn't thought of that. I will consider it."* I immediately follow (in my own head) with, *"they simply don't have all the available facts"*, because this is almost always the case.

There are many people who, with all good intentions, will try to convince you not to do something. Some people do this out of their own fears and others out of a feeling of needing to protect you. In reality, they are trying to protect you from what they fear.

When you start to change the way you think, you will have people around you that will try to pull you back into their own comfort zones. Many times, if others don't understand your new goals or way of thinking, they believe they are helping by trying to stop or restrict you. In other words, bring you around to the way they are thinking.

One of my favorite ways to weed out advice that isn't counsel is to ask a simple question in a soft, friendly, and non-confrontational manner. In my case, it was when I was going into real estate. If someone told me real estate was risky or a bad investment, I would curiously ask, *"How much real estate have you owned?"* In my mind, if someone was going to give me advice on real estate, I would expect them to have owned some real estate.

The answer was usually something like this: *"I don't own any, but I have read about how hard it is to be a landlord."* Another good one was, *"Your money is safer in savings. Are you sure you want to risk it?"* So, I asked, *"If money devalues more than it gains in interest, why is it safer in savings?"* This almost always throws them for a loop.

Advice is useless because it's usually based on personal opinions, not facts or experience. Counsel, on the other hand, comes from those who have experience and are in possession of the facts.

When changing your mindset, seek out people who have the same, or better, mindsets as well as experience. Seek out counsel and ignore advice or opinions. They are useless in reaching your goals.

By seeking counsel, you will increase your useful knowledge, giving yourself the tools to excel. The other benefit to finding other open-minded and experienced people for counsel is that they will support you even if they don't know anything about what it is you are doing. In many cases, they may introduce you to people who do know what they don't know.

Your desires need passion and purpose, but you also need useful knowledge. Your desires are fueled by your passion and your confidence in your desires relies on facts and applicable knowledge.

If you want to own a series of auto repair shops it's best to ask someone who owns an auto repair shop about the business. Don't just ask anyone who has never owned one. Don't ask a mechanic either; he doesn't know what the owner is doing to run his entire business. These people cannot build in you the confidence to have your own auto repair shop, because they are not in possession of the facts on what it actually takes to own a repair shop. When someone doesn't know something, they usually give you opinions that are negative because they don't really know anything about it; they base their opinions on how they feel about it or with incomplete information, either of which is not helpful.

By changing your mindset to seek specific knowledge, generated from a source with real experience, we can grow our own knowledge. Don't just get advice from one source either; no **one** person can have all the knowledge that you might need. While each will have valuable information, your goal is to gather as much information, from as many sources as you can, to benefit you.

There have been many times in my life where I simply changed the way I was thinking, which changed my life. I recommend you think back to your own life to find validation for this aspect of the philosophy.

For example, one time when I was young, I decided to make a change in my life…to act like an adult instead of simply yearning to be one. When I made this change in thinking, I started to become more responsible and those around me treated me as if I were more responsible. In many cases, this will be our parents, first employers, or even associates.

When I started to work my first job at only 14 years old, it didn't go well. I was eventually let go because I wasn't performing the way the manager expected. This was a valuable experience for me because it showed me that I really didn't have an adult mindset.

I didn't know it at the time, but it wasn't until I decided I was going to be more responsible and do exactly what I was told, that my next job would go far better. It didn't take long to find another job. Once I did, I had a new way of thinking about it, a new attitude, so to speak; my next job went much better.

When developing a new way of thinking, we won't achieve anything until we match that new thinking with actions. When working on your new mindset, it's necessary to understand that much of what you will achieve is done by taking action internally -- you will change who you are by changing how you think.

In my coaching business, I was working with a young woman. She was driven, ambitious, and had goals. However, she wasn't progressing towards her goals as she needed to. Instead, she was dwelling on past events that created fears in her mind; she was embracing those fears. They were fears that stopped her from taking actions to move towards her goals. Instead of living in the day, she was focused on the past.

We had many long conversations about certain instances in her life. I spent a lot of time listening, and in doing so, I was able to figure out what was holding her back.

She had several main stories that she told. I immediately recognized that she had been dwelling on these negative stories so much that she had developed mental images in such detail that her focus on those stories were having a negative effect on her thinking. In addition, she was wasting a lot of mental energy developing these elaborate stories in her mind, instead of focusing on her goals.

I asked her what she learned from the events in her life that were positive. She didn't have an answer as she had never tried to put a positive outlook on any of these negative stories. She had spent a lot of time dwelling on the stories and events in her life; so much so that they became a major focus for her. In return for all her dwelling on the negative, she became depressed and full of anxiety.

I told her to share the stories in shorter versions and always end them with what she had learned from the event that could be considered positive. Over a short period of time, we took years of stories and changed her thinking about them.

These very negative stories and thoughts were turned around as she began to accept that there were positive sides to each of her stories. I did this by having her first summarize the negative in the stories and then lose all the elaborate details. These elaborate details took up much of her time and thought process; she was wasting a serious amount of mental energy on them.

Next, she was to finish the story on a positive note. For instance, in one story she felt she had been abused by someone emotionally. She shortened her story to just the main event. Then, I asked her what came from that event that was positive. It went like this:

She had been physically threatened after ignoring her intuition and putting her ambitions ahead of her apprehensions. Now, she realized that had she learned to embrace her intuitions (which were strong) she could have avoided the situation.

I asked her to switch this story up in the way she presented it to others, then think and say to herself something like this:

"I learned how to recognize my intuitions because I ignored them and put myself in a situation in which I was threatened. I'm now grateful this happened because I learned

to start recognizing my intuitions and I can now use that more effectively in the future."

Like many people, she realized that her sixth sense, or intuition, was trying to tell her something that she ignored. There are many instances where people put themselves into bad situations and ignore their sixth sense about it.

You will hear many crime victims say, *"I knew something was going to happen."* This intuition is the universe trying to help you, but many people dismiss it because it isn't logical and can't always be validated. We can't validate this because if we follow that sense of danger, or avoid something to relieve the anxiety, nothing happens. While this is the whole point of the intuition, it provides no validation unless you always follow it and learn the hard way that it was valid.

Sometimes, we have those feelings, but nothing happens so again we can't validate it. Often we ignore them and teach ourselves to believe that our intuitions are false. In many cases, we are not actually using our intuition because it's hard to validate or quantify in a way that gives us faith in it. By changing what you think, and how you feel, you will be readily able to recognize what is actual intuition, but also what opportunities are being presented.

In ancient times, spiritual teachings were part of almost every society's education of children. There was a value put in learning to recognize spiritual ideas, their causes and effects on both the physical world and the unseen world.

The ability to recognize how actions affect our reality, both externally and internally, is a skill held over from childhood. In today's society, it's one we must try to cultivate and, in many cases, re-learn. Many spiritual practices today still recognize this and encourage the belief that the path to happiness must involve the mind as well as our internal beliefs. Happiness is a state of mind not controlled by external events.

When we realize that the law of attraction, the law of increased returns and the other laws of nature are working for us, we can begin to recognize them and see them for what they are; they are the tools by which we create everything in our lives. We attract to us what we put out in our thoughts and we receive what we are asking for in abundance, so be mindful of what you are asking for.

When we dwell on things that make us unhappy, the universe delivers the unhappiness. It doesn't realize you don't want it -- it only sees the visions you are sending to it and responds in kind by delivering more of it.

When we focus on the things that make us happy, we find more happiness coming into our lives. Therefore, when we dwell and meditate on bringing happiness and success into our lives, take actions that allow those things to manifest, we find that we will have happiness and success in our lives.

People who spend a lot of time being lonely can usually be found focusing on the loneliness rather than the potential happiness they will have when they find someone. A simple change in thought will allow someone to take actions towards changing the situation.

Instead of thinking you are lonely, I recommend envisioning the happiness you will have when you find someone. If you are sitting at home on the weekends, contemplating loneliness, focus on something else -- take actions to achieve a different goal. Don't dwell on loneliness or make yourself feel bad because your desire to not be lonely hasn't been fulfilled. Don't focus on finding someone either, instead just know, and have faith, that one day you will find someone to share your happiness with.

Instead of not wanting to be lonely, we should have a desire for companionship and happiness. This simple shift in thinking changes what we are requesting. While this shift doesn't seem all too significant, it truly is. The image we are now sending is that of companionship and happiness. The previous was that of loneliness and unhappiness. Instead of asking not to have something, shift the thoughts to what it is you want, rather than what you don't.

If you think about it, it makes sense. Instead of projecting the image of loneliness you are currently, project the image of happiness and companionship. Instead of saying, "*I don't want loneliness,*" you say, "*I want companionship.*" You are taking a negative thought and turning it into a positive request.

When we start to think about feeling lonely, we should change the thought to something different. This could be our goals, an event we can attend, or new friends with similar mindsets. When we feel good about ourselves, we should perhaps envision sharing our happiness with another person.

By changing this thought process, you can start to attract more positive people into your live. You will eventually meet someone if you truly believe you're going too. By wanting to find someone to share your success and happiness, you will find someone to share with.

This works for far more then loneliness. We can apply this methodology to everything we want. Don't dwell on what you don't want; instead dwell on things you *do* want and know you will have them.

The affirmation that you already have these things sends those positive feelings, beliefs and thoughts out into the universe. If you have the mindset of success and happiness, the universe will have no choice but to deliver those things to you; clouding them with negative thoughts, self-doubt, or anxiety will inhibit your ability to receive the things you desire. This happens because your focus isn't on finding the things you want, instead it's on avoiding the things you don't want.

Changing the way you think goes far beyond just the esoteric because your thoughts control your actions and allow you to recognize and act on opportunities that involve all the aspects of your life. To change our careers, we have to do the work and believe that we can change our careers. If you want to do like I have done and become a teacher, mentor and coach, then you have to do the work. You have to believe that you are a teacher, mentor, and coach. If you want to find a partner to share your life with, then you have to believe you will find that person.

When I made the decision to start coaching, I immediately started by telling people what I was doing. I didn't say, *"I think I'm going to be,"* or *"I'm working on being a coach."* When someone asked me about my job, or what it was I did, I would respond without hesitation, *"I'm a personal improvement coach, author, and real estate investor."*

After all, I had done a lot of the work. I had the knowledge and knew the philosophy I was using to coach very well. I had studied the philosophies, and I had already done a lot of coaching and mentoring. Therefore, I was already doing what I said I was doing. You can do the same thing -- just believe that you are already what you want to be, and put in the work to go to the next level to achieve it.

I realized that, without even trying, I had already been developing myself for more than two decades. I knew what my dreams were; I just needed to start doing those things.

Once I did this, and followed my own teachings, I entirely changed my life. I was a professional coach, an author, and even a real estate investor. There is no lying or deception involved when you are doing what you say you are doing. Build the groundwork, set your foundations, and then go to the next level. The universe had already lined me up for this. It just took a change in thinking to believe in myself and reach my own dreams and goals.

In a short period of time, I went from wishing and dreaming to actually taking action and doing more to grow those aspects of my life. The change in mindset brought these things into my life very quickly. Looking back, I wonder why I didn't start sooner.

The only answer I had was that it took all the setbacks, failures, and adversity to teach me how I was going to achieve these things. They gave me the experience I now draw upon to help others. All those obstacles were turned into the wisdom and experience that I can now reflect on and share with others to help elevate them to new higher levels of happiness and success.

All the setbacks, failures, and adversities were the seeds that would allow me to grow the wisdom and experience to become what I am today. Your own setbacks happen for a reason, so never look on them as failures. Instead, learn from them and move forward as a stronger person. When you are ready to recognize why and how they benefit you, you will be able to move beyond them. You will be able to see your own fortitude, appreciate the challenges and build faith and trust in yourself.

I learned to be happy and content in the moment, but never satisfied. Being content is in the now, and satisfaction is granted only in the future. By being happy, grateful, and content in the present, we create the positive energy we need to feed our desires and reach our goals.

Our desires feed our need for satisfaction; however, being content and grateful right now, with what you have, gives you the positive attitude needed to move forward. I say this because if you become completely satisfied with life as it is, you will be unable to achieve more. So, be happy and content today, but always strive for satisfaction tomorrow.

Once you master this concept, your desires will build to obsessive heights. Your goals will constantly increase, and you will be happy because you are content in the moment.

When I started telling people I was a coach, it was only days until I had my first professional student. In the beginning, I would exchange services for coaching and take on friends who were truly interested in my teachings for free. I did this because I was aware that I could grow from every experience and hone my skills in coaching. The more I honed my skills the better coach I would be. I never settle for just getting by, and neither should you.

Once I was focused on this path, everything came to me easily. I simply believed in what I was, took actions to achieve those goals, and became what it was I desired to be. Once the decision was made, it was all done in a very short period of time.

Though it may seem like an "overnight" success to some, it actually took three decades of learning and work to achieve it. It wasn't until I changed my mindset that things actually started to happen; it wasn't until I reviewed my own past and associations in extreme detail that I was able to develop my own system. Having a plan is part of that system, and without a plan we can never achieve anything because we have nothing to strive for. Make your plan and work towards your goals constantly.

While you probably don't want to be a coach, it's likely you have some desire that you haven't achieved yet. Otherwise, you probably wouldn't be reading this book or seeking guidance.

Whatever your desires are, change your mindset from wishing and dreaming to one of definite intent and desires to achieve, and then take actions towards reaching those goals every day. You do this by developing a plan, acting on it and knowing it will happen.

Dreams that are put in motion by developing a plan become a goal. Put the Three Horses of your mind to work and hone the skills needed to work for you. You can only change who you are by changing the way you think. Change the way you think and feel about yourself and your reality, and you will find success.

Your Balance Sheet

GIVING, RECEIVING AND MORE

The idea of a balance sheet in life is nothing new. Most of us understand the concept of karma. There have been 1000's of books written on the subject which try to explain karma and how it affects your life. Karma is usually seen as a system in nature that controls what it is that comes into your life. When you do positive things, you receive positive back into your life. When you do negative things, you bring negativity into your life.

Karma works in conjunction with the law of attraction. I like to call it your "balance sheet", which is constantly calculating your worth. The value you bring to others should always be more than what you intend to charge. This increases your balance sheet; the more value you show on your balance sheet, the better the returns.

I take the concept of having a balance sheet seriously. There are aspects to your balance sheet that you may be unaware of. One of the greatest aspects constantly overlooked is the relationship between giving and receiving.

In order to give, you must also be willing to receive. Even if this seems to be the opposite of what we are taught, it is very much true. There was a valuable lesson I learned in recent years, one that is very important to finding happiness and success. This lesson sounds simple: **You must be willing to receive**. However, most of us don't understand the need to receive and, in fact, feel selfish when receiving.

I always felt I could do everything for myself. I never liked help from anyone, unless there was no other choice. Now, I don't hesitate to allow someone to help me out. I would be guilty of robbing them of the pleasure and positive response from the universe by denying them the ability to be generous and giving. Until I was willing to receive, I wasn't able to recognize all the wonderful gifts that the universe was trying to give me.

My attitude of "I can do everything for myself", my guilt about receiving, and my denying others the ability to give were all inhibiting my ability to recognize those gifts. Though I was generous to others, I wasn't allowing others to be generous to me. My balance sheet was out of whack. I had a very long column of giving with almost nothing on the receiving side, unless I was at a point of desperation.

This desperation to receive was being created by my lack of grateful receiving in the first place. Gratefulness is another key mindset to have. We should be grateful for everything in our lives. If you're not grateful, then why would anyone want to go out of their way for you? Especially, why would the universe want to?

Many of us are raised with the belief that giving is honorable, and it is, but at that same time, we learn that receiving isn't unnecessary or even negative. There is a problem with this. If you want to be able to give to someone, you must be willing to receive. If not, there will be no one left for you to give to.

This doesn't mean you can sit around and have the world handed to you on a platter; that type of receiving is disempowering and creates laziness in your life. It allows for many distractions and negativity to manifest around you. It isn't even real receiving, it is taking.

Confusing a sense of entitlement with the willingness to receive has a negative result in your life. If we take advantage of another person's generosity, then we will create negativity in our own lives. Taking advantage of others is not positive. Taking should never be confused with receiving.

When we change our minds about our own entitlements, we begin to realize that we need to return everything that is given to us. Once we start to return more than we were given, we can reap the benefits of receiving.

I'm talking about receiving from others and recognizing opportunities that are trying to help you achieve your goals. The universe will deliver opportunities if your desires are focused and the powers of your mind are harnessed properly. You must practice gratitude for what you are receiving and a willingness to receive it.

Receiving for me was harder than giving. I had to learn to receive as well as improve my way of giving. I have always been grateful for what I have, but my unwillingness to receive was limiting where I could go.

Simple acts of kindness are a great way of giving, and they are also a great way of receiving. I had some serious issues in receiving direct help from others in the past. I wasn't willing to receive because I felt that receiving was wrong and selfish.

I believed that I needed do everything myself, which only made the matter worse. I never wanted to be a burden to others who might want to take the time or effort to help me. In addition, I had a negative view of people who received constantly. I did all of this with no regard to those who were giving, or the benefits they would receive from giving.

I was putting a negative spin on people giving to me while robbing them of the chance to help. None of this was intentional, but there is one simple fact about giving and receiving: if no one is willing to receive, then no one will be able to give. If we take this to the extreme, then the only people left to give to are the takers, and they do not return the favors to others.

It's pretty easy to spot the takers who have no gratitude for what they are receiving. Many of them never get anywhere in life as they become dependent on the givers for everything they have.

Seeing a lack of gratitude is a sure means of spotting people who take without returning the generosity. This is often seen in the entitlement mindset. The belief is that somehow one deserves something for nothing and returns nothing for what is received, not even gratitude. The key to receiving in a positive way is gratitude. If you receive with gratitude you will return the favors one day. Gratitude is the means by which we return what it is we have received.

Since being generous and giving have so many positive effects on the person doing it, it's truly wrong to deny them this pleasure and the positive benefits of giving. Don't rob people of the opportunity to reap the benefits of giving by denying their help. In turn, ensure that you return their generosity to all those around you.

True giving isn't always about money, it's about sharing all the things you have in life, especially knowledge. Although having money helps when it comes time to give, it's not your only valuable asset. By being wealthy you can give more to others, not only because you have more money to give, but also because you usually have extra time to give. You will be able to share the knowledge of how you became successful. If you're a generous person, then being wealthy will allow you to be more generous.

There are some problems with giving, especially when it comes to money. Giving money can be a wonderful thing, provided it's going to good use. If you give money to someone who will buy drugs with it, you are making the problem worse. If you give money to a homeless family that needs a place to live, then your money is being put to good use.

Knowing when to give money can be more difficult than you imagine. People know that we inherently don't want to give money for drugs or alcohol, so they may lie and tell you they are buying food. We still give, even though we may know we are being lied to. Many people avoid this by giving to trusted charities, but many charities are only giving a small portion to their causes. In any case, when you give, do your best to know who and what you are giving money to and where it's going.

If you exercise caution in giving then you are doing your best to ensure your charity is going to a good cause, to truly help someone. When your goals are to be successful and people help you, they are helping someone who's grateful and will return the generosity.

Knowing who your friends are, and how much they respect you, is also important. This is because we tend to be more charitable in our own circles. We feel we know those people so our charity will be used wisely and for good.

If you loan a friend money and you are repaid, great. If this person continues to ask for more favors, but never repays them, or gets angry when you eventually refuse, then this person is not your friend.

This may sound cold, but people will either respect you for whom and what you are, or they won't. If they don't respect you, it will be obvious if you're paying attention. Simply refuse to do a favor -- you will immediately know this person only likes you for what you can give them and not who you are. If they continue to be friends with you, then it's likely they still respect you.

There are many people who will try to take advantage of you. If you control who you give to, how it is given, and when you give, you can control the number of times you are abused through your own generosity. When we give and the return is abuse, we tend to become less willing to give. When we trust, without having first tested the relationship, and become the victim, it's our own fault. We have done no "due diligence" on the friendship or relationship. While this may seem unnecessary at first, it's actually very necessary to our own long-term outlook on the subject of giving.

It's very easy to fall into the trap of feeling negative about giving. When we are taken advantage of, and we feel abused, we can become cold and less willing to give. By monitoring who it is we are generous to, we can control the outcome and keep our positive outlook on giving.

I find it best to keep your direct giving only to very close friends and associates who have proven that they respect you. You can also give to total strangers who can't come back to you over and over again.

Additionally, I found that when I went the extra mile (which is a form of giving) for an employer that didn't appreciate it, finding a new job with someone who did paid great dividends.

If your employer doesn't appreciate you, then find one who will. Don't sit around complaining about your situation; change it so that you can be of service to someone who will benefit you. Find someone who respects you for who you are, not simply what you're doing for them.

On the advice of my mentor, I started to pick up pennies and give thanks for the gift. Showing and having gratitude is important, you should always give thanks for everything you have and receive. After all, the universe is giving you a gift and will appreciate your gratefulness, thereby giving you more. This is part of having a money mindset and seeing the opportunities lain out before you.

Eventually I started to find more loose change; I now find dimes regularly. Just recently, I bent down to pick up a penny and just out of sight was a dime. The gifts have increased as I have more gratitude and a willingness to accept those gifts. While it may seem small, it's about the mindset and willingness to receive, combined with having gratitude for the gift.

When we look at all aspects of receiving, the more grateful we are for what we have and the more we seem to get. Having gratitude is truly a great thing, and giving back is the sincere form of gratitude.

The ability to return everything to someone else is where the real gold is in receiving. The more you receive, the more you should give, and the more positive energy you will receive in return for your generosity. This continues to build up your balance sheet and creates more abundance in your life. If you just drain others by constantly receiving and never giving, your balance sheet becomes out of balance.

Giving and being gracious helps regulate your balance sheet with the universe. Eventually if you fail to give and fail to have gratitude for what you are receiving, you wear down this balance.

The law of economics, increased returns and attraction all come into play when you are both receiving and giving. If you feel you are entitled to something, then you will only receive what others are either willing or forced to give you.

No one is entitled to anything. If you believe that you are, these philosophies will not work for you. These philosophies require that you be responsible for yourself and be generous. You should try to return all that you have been given, and more, in one form or another.

The Law of Economics states that nothing is free; someone has to pay for it. If you feel you are entitled to something, then you are violating the law of economics. If you give the extra effort, and do everything you can to repay the generosity given to you by being generous in return, you can reap the benefits of your efforts. You will be doing the right things to build your balance sheet in a positive way.

We can give in many ways. I feel that helping people grow, become successful and happy in life are the greatest gifts you can give. If you realize that all you need to do to receive positivity is to return the generosity of others in a positive way, receiving becomes much more beneficial and rewarding. Receiving becomes a positive influence in your life because you are also returning to others what you have already received. If you are already receiving, then good for you, but please ensure that you return the gifts to others so you will have no problems with your balance sheet.

The balance sheet contains several features of your own personality and actions. Some call it karma, but whatever you call it, it is real and does play a role in your life. By recognizing the balance sheet of life, we can envision what it is we have on our sheet.

Every interaction we have with the universe, and others, carries with it some form of balance -- the Ying &Yang so to speak -- the positive and negative energies we send out and receive from the universe. This balance is easy to maintain with a small amount of effort, but we must have the recognition that we have a balance sheet in the first place if we ever wish to maintain it.

This balance will affect your ability to control your horses, or the powers of your mind. If your balance sheet is off, your ability to control your horses through positivity is affected.

If you become greedy and self-centered, your goals then become selfish. This abuse will eventually come calling, as the laws of the universe do not bend for anyone. Greed generally leads to destruction because it's an out of control passion.

Greed in any aspect of life leads us down a path of negativity. Many people confuse wanting to be rich or wealthy with greed. There is a difference between being wealthy simply for the gain of money and being wealthy in order to achieve certain goals. Being wealthy so that you may be more generous and live life in such a way as to enjoy the ultimate freedoms life has to offer is positive. If, on the other hand, you simply want power and money, then your desires for wealth become destructive and negative.

There is a long list of people who approached wealth with the idea of greed and had their lives destroyed by it. Simply do a search on the internet for "millionaires who went to jail" and a long list of examples will show up.

In reviewing this list you will see that in almost every case, it was an abuse of power -- or greed for money -- that ended up destroying them. Remember, money doesn't make you something; it only enhances what you already are.

There are several facets to maintaining your balance sheet that we should pay close attention to. First is the relationship between positive and negative energies that we project into the universe. These are directly influenced by our positive and negative actions and thoughts. We should constantly try to be aware of the results of our actions and do our best to ensure that the end results of our actions are positive.

Another item you should find regularly on your balance sheet is that of helping others. While this is part of giving and receiving, I want to ensure that you are aware of the magnitude of its importance. Helping others is a key to your success. The people who have helped society the most have also gained the most. They gave of themselves with their time and determination, sometimes waiting for decades before actually starting to receive anything in return.

Most overnight successes have actually had many years of struggles behind them, which eventually made them an *"overnight"* success. This is key to understanding the effort, persistence and time that it takes to develop and reach goals of great magnitude. Understand that of all of the setbacks that come to pass are preparing you for your success. This becomes obvious once you start to have your own success, but without this preparation, you will likely be unable to hold on to your success and it will be short lived.

I went through years of financial struggles, rarely ever having enough money to do the basic things I wanted. I drove used, worn-out cars and rarely ever took a break. While I did own a few nice things during those times, they came at great cost to me.

The lessons learned during my hard times are now benefiting me greatly. I learned to manage money and I'm still a good money manager. I understand the value of saving to obtain something, while ensuring that what I do obtain is worth the cost. If you have experienced, or still are experiencing, a life of scarcity, be grateful. If you never have had to live off scarcity, you should also be grateful. Be grateful for the lessons you learned firsthand, or the ones others shared with you to help you avoid having to learn the hard way.

Had I never been through the financial struggles that I went through, it would be harder for me to handle money today. I may not be able to recognize the value in what I can do to help people, had I never been through similar hardships.

Whatever lessons life has taught you, it's done so for a reason, and it's up to you to find those reasons. The universe knows exactly what you need to learn. In reality, most people don't find the lessons at the moment they are taught. It isn't until later, once we have changed our mindset that we start to understand those lessons. By being a thinker and going through the process of applying clear thinking to your past and present, you will be able to find the lessons and grow from them.

If, at the time of those lessons, we have a positive outlook on our lives, we would have learned those lessons quicker. This is why the horses of our minds need a positive mindset behind them. Without it, they can't carry or guide you, and you will miss the lessons life is trying to teach you. While you may not see the benefits when a setback comes to you, they are there. If you focus on finding them, you will.

If you want your balance sheet to be positive, you may want to try finding the positive in life. Dwelling on only the negatives creates more negativity and messes up your balance sheet. Striving for money alone will not deliver the money to you. If your goal is monetary gain, helping people is a sure way of finding it. As I have said before, if you base your success solely on monetary gain, you may find it hard to have any.

Your balance sheet is with you always. You can't disregard it, nor can you ignore it. It's always calculating and always delivers exactly what you put into it. The balance sheet involves each of the laws of nature. In the end, it's the final tally of your actual worth. All negativity lowers your balance sheet while positivity adds to it.

As said before, your horses do not respond to negativity, which even has the ability to bring you to a complete halt, therefore stopping you from ever achieving your goals. There is no magic that can change the laws of the universe, no matter how hard you try.

What you believe when it comes to the laws of nature doesn't change them. We can't ignore them; we must use them to our advantage. The proof of these laws and the effect of our balance sheet exist all around us. If you truly look, you will find that nearly everything in a person's life is traced to an attitude or belief that the person has.

Your balance sheet is there whether you believe it or not. Simply know it's there, put the positive thoughts and actions into it. Give and allow others to give to you so they too can enjoy the rewards of giving. Operate with purpose and not out of greed, helping others along the way. Be good to other people and bring with you a positive outlook to every challenge you meet.

Going the Extra Mile

INCREASING LIFE'S RETURNS

One of the main reasons we need to cover this a little more is that it's important to understand the benefits in going the extra mile. Remember that people won't like you for what you give them; they will like you for who you are. If someone likes you simply for what you can give them, then they are not worth closely associating with.

To go the extra mile simply means you are doing more than what you are being paid for or more than is expected of you. When you go the extra mile, you will benefit from the law of increased returns. This law of nature states that you will receive more than you give in return when you work with all the laws of nature. Going the extra mile should be done to benefit others. While you will benefit in the long term from doing this, the driving force should be kindness and consideration.

To enjoy the benefits of going the extra mile, we must first realize that it doesn't create friendships or loyalties. In most cases, those expecting this outcome are going to be disappointed. Bear this in mind when you go the extra mile for people; if someone doesn't respect you for who you are, doing favors and going the extra mile for them will usually end up in disappointment. You want to be worth more than you charge, or receive, for services.

How does one go the extra mile without finding disappointment? First, try not to have expectations and do things simply for the joy of benefiting others. Second, don't continue with a false thought that someone is going to gain respect for you if you keep doing things for them, this will never happen. People who don't respect you for who you are will not change simply because you do something for them.

In order to fully benefit from going the extra mile and harnessing the Law of Increased returns we need to understand how they work. In nature we see the law of increased returns in action regularly. The farmer plants one seed and gets hundreds back. We can plant one corn seed and then we will get one or two complete ears. The more we master this law, the greater the returns are. The corn farmer can plant acres of fields and harvest enough corn to feed hundreds of cattle and people all year. One man can provide for hundreds -- that's a serious return on his investment of knowledge and time.

The farmer puts his knowledge of the rules of nature regarding corn to work for him. He gives all his efforts, puts up his own money, fuels his tractor, and plants the seeds. He knows that the rules of nature will give him the returns he needs and desires. He also understands that nature sometimes deals us setbacks in the form of a bad crop or stormy growing season.

The well-prepared farmer understands that he must also recognize that setbacks are part of nature, and do occur. So he has insurance, back up funds, and other safeguards for these events. No farmer will plant a bag of old expired seeds expecting a full crop. Nor should you plant damaged seeds expecting anything in return.

Much like the farmer, we grow what we plant, and what we receive is based on our knowledge and understanding of the rules. The old adage "*We reap what we sow*" is a true statement. We see the bees collect pollen and know that the yield from their tireless work will be a bounty of honey far greater than they will ever need.

If we take these examples and apply them to ourselves, the rules of nature don't change. You get more than you give, provided that you are patient and play by the rules.

In today's society there seems to be a belief that life is fair by default. There is no equity simply for equities sake. If you don't give, you won't receive; if you don't play by the rules you will not succeed. This shouldn't stop you from giving more before you receive in the form of going the extra mile. This also shouldn't stop you from receiving when the opportunities arise. All aspects of this philosophy work together in harmony.

We see this simple rule that *"the game isn't fair"* play out all through life. Man creating fairness is an illusion; the only fairness is adhering to the rules. If you play by the rules, you will reap the rewards. If you do not, you will reap the losses, and if you view this as unfair, then it is. If however, we discern that in reality, it is fair because everyone has the same opportunity to play by the rules then we can benefit by those rules. Therefore, in my mind, it is fair because it's up to the individual to make things happen for him/herself.

In the business world, this rule applies more harshly. The rules are not fair; therefore, we have to learn how to play by them in order to succeed. Remember the tattoo studio that was shut down because I didn't follow the rules? That is a perfect example of having to play by the rules.

No one will refund your money on the stock market if you make a mistake. Regulations that could ruin your business are in place, whether fair or not. It is up to you to play by those rules or you will lose that game. There are rules all through life, both man-made and enforced by nature; each needs to be adhered to. If you don't play by them you end up on the losing side.

In the end, though, this can all be viewed as fair because these same rules apply to everyone. Those who go around the rules are irrelevant; their balance sheet will eventually take care of them.

If you are not giving more than you are receiving, you have exactly what it is you deserve and you're probably already receiving more than you have earned.

In order to prove the idea of going the extra mile, you need only to become an observer of life. The fruit trees bear enough fruit to feed the animals and propagate the surrounding species. They give a bounty every year by simply growing flowers, fruit, and seeds. Once nature takes its course, the bounty is abundant.

In the case of trees, they have long lives and can survive several bad seasons and still stay alive. Nature has created a balance. Therefore, the trees give far more than they need to propagate their species. In return, they are given a lifespan that far exceeds those that receive their bounty.

In the past, humans harvested trees and let nature take care of the rest. When people began to feel we were over-harvesting the trees, they looked to the laws of nature for an answer. Whether realizing it or not, they tried to create a balance by giving back what they were receiving. In most areas today, humans replant the forest after harvest, or only harvest a certain percentage of the trees, thus allowing nature to restore its bounty.

We gained knowledge through experience that by replanting the forest we decrease the time it takes for trees to repopulate. Our harvesting today has little impact on the environment. We are smart enough and have given enough back that we have made trees a renewable resource. We also found that by removing the older growth, younger, healthier growth comes up, renewing the forest and keeping the cycle going.

If you look at any fruiting plant, it always returns more than it takes to grow or propagate the species. Squash plants produce dozens of squashes from just one seed. The same goes for tomatoes, beans, peas, peppers, and most all other plants we enjoy for our own sustenance.

In return, the greatest producers become protected. We purposefully protect the heartiest, most bountiful plants and save their seeds to aid in their propagation. The greater the bounty they produce, the more likely we are to shelter them to ensure their continuation.

Some plants provide humans with nothing but beauty, but when we look closely, we find that they are providing more to other aspects of nature, such as pollen for bees or food for smaller life forms. So the plants *are* still providing food in some form.

I have gone the extra mile nearly my entire life to move up in both the private and business worlds. I have always made myself available, done extra work, and been willing to do whatever it was that needed to be done. If I wanted to move up in the companies which I worked for, going the extra mile was always a sure means of being recognized. In addition, it feels good to go out of your way and help solve problems or lend an extra hand.

You can do this too. If you're willing to go the extra mile, you will increase your value. When you increase your value, you don't just want more from life, you demand more, and the universe will deliver it to you.

From my experience, those who view others going the extra mile as kiss-ups don't actually go the extra mile so don't see the value in it. At the same time, many who do go the extra mile don't even realize the actual benefits of doing so. They just inherently know it's the right thing to do and do it. Once someone realizes that the extra effort pays both internally in positive feelings and as an increase in their balance sheet, they continue to do it.

While some may not realize it, what they are doing is using the law of increased returns to better themselves and their lives. We receive good feelings for doing this first, and then we receive the benefits through increased returns.

In the future, opportunities will be laid before you because of your increased balance sheet. The returns for going the extra mile are well worth the effort; you won't need to think about them. These are the rules, and the universe always plays by its own rules.

We may not know how, or where, the universe will repay us for our efforts, but it will happen. If you have your plan, your major purpose, and you play by the rules, the universe will know exactly where its repayment should take place. By building your plan, you tell the universe where payment is due. In addition, those around you will also know of your plans and help you to achieve them.

You are planting the seed, watering it and waiting for the returns to come to you. Not unlike the farmer, once you understand these rules of increased returns, you can relax and let nature return the abundance you have asked for.

This is why we can make demands of the universe and receive its abundance and bounty. Like the farmer, we can only reap what we sow; if we don't work the field, there is no possibility of returns. The laws of nature require you to give the extra effort to reap the rewards.

If we do nothing and still have food, shelter, and clothing, then we are already receiving an overabundance of returns. By observing yourself and others, we can see the universe continually giving more than what people put into it. In some cases, so much is given to those who break the rules of economics that there is animosity by those who don't understand the rules.

Those who do nothing, never go the extra mile, whose only efforts are to demand more for less while making continual demands of the universe are doomed to spiritual and personal poverty. The only reason they have what they do is because of the rules that permit it. If we demand more than we give, the law of economics will eventually collapse around us. We must give to receive and stay in balance, those are the rules. When the balance sheet becomes too far out of balance, nature will correct itself.

We can see this balance happen before our own eyes. If we look at the old forest, where new growth can't take place, dead trees are lying along the ground, standing dead, reaching up to the sky. Eventually, nature sends a lightning bolt and burns the forest to the ground. By destroying what is no longer giving, nature allows for new growth to spring up and provide the abundance and bounty it demands of all life.

This cycle is true everywhere in life; humans are no exception. If an animal gets out of control and destroys its own food source it will perish. A perfect example is the locust swarm which devours everything in its path. The locust starts to starve and dies off when nothing is left. Parasites that are out of control kill the host, in turn, killing themselves and their ability to reproduce. Viruses have the same problem. They become so efficient at taking they kill both the host and themselves. The rules are everywhere you look and are put into observable practice.

If we don't return more to the world than is expected, and continually go the extra mile, we too will perish. Those who don't go the extra mile will eventually loose and live in poverty, be it financially, emotionally or spiritually. They will use up all the resources available to them because they are creating nothing and giving nothing in return. Eventually, the law of economics kicks in and burns all that is useless.

There is no escaping the rules, and those who master the mare are like the new growth in the forest. Accordingly, abundance is provided to them in return. By giving abundantly, we are rewarded with even more abundance. Not enough can be said about the symbiotic relationships in life between the laws of nature. The law of economics, the law of attraction and the law of increased returns work in perfect harmony. As do all the other laws of nature, everything that breaks the laws eventually will perish or live in some form of poverty.

The universe and nature are not heartless; they do have compassion. Nature lets things go for a very long time before calling in the balance sheets. We have the ability to recognize the effects we have on our environment. We are the only species that can actively change our environment for the better, but we can also change it for the worse. In either case, nature will find a way to balance everything.

When I was growing up, I had two experiences which illustrated this. One was of an older woman who was handicapped. She wasn't completely disabled, but she walked with a cane and had to live on assistance. She spent her time volunteering at the church; she always had a smile and a kind word to say.

She continually offered help, even baked cookies for the church and neighborhood kids on occasion; everyone seemed to love her. Each holiday, family and friends brought a feast to her home. Although she never wanted anything, she continually had the support of her neighbors, friends, and family. She constantly gave of herself in positive words and actions. She gave all she could and in return, everyone was willing to help her out. She wasn't a burden on anyone; instead, it was a joy for people to help her out when she needed it.

Just down the street was another family, with six children living in the home, on assistance. The place was a wreck and it smelled bad. Mom and Dad were both alcoholics and outright lazy. They did nothing but take -- they didn't even properly raise their own children. As a child, I was friends with one of their kids. I always felt bad for them. We could hear the parents fighting regularly. They never went to work; it seemed drinking and doing nothing were their only goals.

The rewards for this lack of effort were obvious. They lived in a dirty, poverty-stricken home and several of their children became lifelong criminals. They never gave or appreciated what they had. Instead, they ended up destroying all around them.

They blamed everyone but themselves for their plight. They expected the world to deliver, but never appreciated the help they were given. They never gave back, which, in turn, caused them to be viewed as nuisances to the entire neighborhood. When I say that your mind creates your reality, these are two examples of just that.

In one last story, I will tell you of the meanest bully I ever met in my life. I was going into 8th grade and my parents had just gotten divorced. I moved in with my father, for various reasons. He was a teacher at the high school while I was in the middle school. I made a few friends over summer break, but the school was new to me and I didn't know what was what or who was who. During a lunch period at the start of the school year, a boy much larger than me demanded that I hand over my lunch.

He was more than 10 inches taller than me (or at least that's how I remember him). Scared, but holding it in, I looked him in the eye and said *"No! And if you touch it, I'll have you kicked out of school for stealing it."* Well, he did anyway. He grabbed it and walked away. In my mind I wasn't going to spend the next five years being bullied by this jerk, so I walked straight to the lunch room monitor. She caught him eating my pudding at the table. He was suspended for five days; however, the story doesn't end there, as I'm sure you expected.

A couple of days later, two friends who had warned me of the wrath of this bully were walking home from school with me. All of a sudden, out of nowhere, my books went flying out of my hands. This monster of a kid screamed at me,

*"You got me suspended and now I'm going to kick your a**."*

*"I'm not the f****** thief who got suspended,"* I responded, *"You are."*

Punches started landing hard on me. The worst beating of my life had just commenced. I tried to hit back, but his arms were long and he was simply a much better fighter. I was going to take everything this punk could deliver. My hands went up and I started to endure the beating.

He beat me so badly that he lost any sort of positive relationship he had with most students in the school, including his own circle. His true cruelty was on display that day and his merciless behavior was highlighted by his brutal actions. In a final act of utter disdain for my indiscretions and being brave enough to endure the beating, he kicked me between the legs to finally drop me. The other kids watching were in shock as I lay there, swollen and bleeding, a lump on the ground.

It took weeks for all the wounds to heal. He had fractured my nose and knocked several of my teeth loose. There wasn't a spot on my cheeks that weren't swollen or bleeding. My ribs hurt, and my lower parts were not happy about the whole thing either.

My father later pressed me for the name of who beat me. He already knew who it was because he had been informed of the lunch room situation. I didn't say -- there was childhood honor at stake here. I licked my wounds, and to the amazement of my classmates, returned to school the following Monday.

I wasn't the only one he went after over the next five years. He pursued everyone who dared to challenge his childhood authority. He also beat a couple of my other friends senselessly. With each beating, kids were standing up to him more and more. Soon, the notion that he had any sort of power over us began to diminish.

He still found people to pick on and bully; it was obvious he was gaining his own self-worth from his treatment of others. He was so ruthless and intolerable that people still remember his behavior to this day. What a sad thing to be remembered for.

There was a positive lesson I learned from this experience though: I realized that I was tough; I didn't have to take anything from anyone. That bully never touched me again. After that year, I hit a growth spurt and bulked up a bit working on my uncle's farm during the summer. I wasn't a frail, easy target anymore. I always assumed he knew I could take it and didn't want to find out if I could dish it out. He never touched me again, as I was big enough to fight back and I think he knew it. Like all bullies, the weak were his targets. This series of events empowered and strengthened my self-esteem. Instead of focusing just on anger and rage, I used the experience to my advantage.

I was never bullied by anyone in that school again. The day I confronted the bully still lingers with me as an empowering event in my life, not something belittling or disempowering. I instead drew power from it. I turned the beating of a lifetime into something positive.

When I was discharged from the military, I ran into this bully once again. He was at a pub sitting alone at the bar. He was no longer the hulking muscular boy I remembered. Maybe he never was, maybe it was my internal perceptions of him fed by my fears.

He was now a reflection of his past behavior. Sitting lonely at a bar stool with a cheap draft beer in front of him, half drunk in the afternoon, he was dressed in what looked like an auto mechanic's outfit. He looked grimy and smelled rather unpleasant, like grease and a long day's hard work. He immediately recognized me, almost as if we were friends, and said:

"Hey Todd, how are you? I heard you were in the service and served in the gulf war?"

"Yes, I did."

As I turned to walk away, I glanced back at him. In a somber voice, I said, *"Best of luck to you."* I truly felt pity for the lonely bully who had gathered the fruits of his past behavior. His balance sheet was obviously coming due.

It was this chance encounter with a man who ruled the world during his teen years, through cruelty and abuse that led me to conclude he was now seeing the returns of having alienated himself from those he abused. He abused his power and ability to beat people, and engaged in cruelty. Instead of being honorable, defending the weak, he beat the powerless. Instead of being someone trustworthy, he used his size to take what he wanted from others.

This man's balance sheet had come due. He had started his reign of terror as a child and now, as an adult, his life was ruined by his cruelty and abusive behavior. Had he taken some lessons from those he abused, he might have learned something. If he knew that being good to others would make you happy and bring great rewards, he might have been able to change.

He had it within his power *then* to change, and even today he is balancing his sheet. He only needed to start doing the right thing, rather than indulging in self-pity over his situation and burying himself at the local pub. I don't know what became of him; I can only hope that he somehow found a way out and has had a happy life.

Our balance sheet continually calculates our worth in the universe, and your returns are increased both good and bad. Make sure you keep your worth high so you can draw in the benefits of life. There is no surer way to be defeated than to be selfish in your treatment of others. Instead, go the extra mile. Go out of your way to help others.

Give openly and generously. If you don't have money, share your experiences and a positive attitude to help lift others up. Grow from setbacks and challenges rather than pitying yourself for having them in the first place. Increase your balance sheet daily, and soon, you will reap the rewards. When we go the extra mile for others, we can correct any imbalance on our sheet, and we can see the changes almost immediately. If you change your frowns to smiles you immediately start to see the change in those around you. If you start doing these small things today, you will see the change sooner than later.

Going the extra mile is about being the one who can be depended on, the one who smiles and finds the good in nearly everything. Going the extra mile isn't just about what you do, but how you do it. Do everything with a positive outlook and be genuinely happy about being able to do it.

Going the extra mile for *you* is just as important as going the extra mile for others. When you are going the extra mile for yourself, you will make things happen. Many people get hung up in old patterns of thought, or bad mental habits, refusing to improve themselves. If you are conscious of the idea of going the extra mile for others, you should ensure you do it for yourself also.

If you are presented with an opportunity, but decide to give it up so that you won't be inconvenienced, you are actually failing to go the extra mile for yourself. Usually, going the extra mile requires some form of sacrifice. We sometimes have to give up leisure time, put in extra work and studies during our down times -- whatever the case, go the extra mile for yourself and others.

When you go the extra mile for yourself, try to keep in mind that your attitude about it must be positive. Don't view it as dreadful or dreary; approach everything you do for yourself and others in good spirits. Enjoy the process and the process becomes easier. It is absolutely worth it.

Mastermind

TEAMING UP IN THOUGHT

Mastermind: When 2 or more people work together in perfect harmony to work towards a singular goal.

The mastermind principle is fairly simple: Form alliances with those who are like-minded. Find quality people with whom you can share ideas, enhance your life, and mutually prosper; you prosper more together than you would separately. Build a team of two, or more, whose goals are to reach whatever goal the founder of the mastermind has.

When we work in perfect harmony, we increase the powers of our minds by making them a single mind. Each is working towards the same goal. All ideas are geared towards helping the leader of the mastermind group reach their goals. It's important to understand that those invited into the mastermind must be selfless and in complete support of the founder. In addition, they should all be of the highest character and true, quality people.

It's the founder's responsibility to return all they can to those in the group who help them. This singular focus and joint definiteness of purpose is where the power in a true mastermind comes from. The group shares the intent and works together to make it reality. In return, the entire group benefits by receiving the rewards of the founder's success.

When you put two or more minds together, the power of both minds is increased exponentially. The first time I experienced a mastermind was with my wife. Although I didn't realize it at first, each time we had a goal, we worked it out together. We found solutions, presented ideas, and solved countless problems. As time went on, our private little mastermind group was getting some serious results.

There is a difference between cooperation and an actual mastermind alliance. The mastermind works in perfect harmony, there is no negativity or animosity. The goal is laid out. All parties involved are aware that the singular goal is the sole focus and intent of the mastermind group. Cooperation alone is powerful; a true mastermind is unstoppable.

To show how cooperation turned into a mastermind, I will tell you another story from my personal journey. During the peak of the Great Recession of 2008, I lost my job. About a month later, my wife also lost her job. I was on unemployment when she lost her job.

We had just bought a house a few months earlier. The market for jobs was extremely weak. We had a nice house, two cars, and a really comfortable life. Sadly, this was all about to change and test our fortitude as a couple and in life.

After putting out nearly 300 resumes, I had only one interview. No one was hiring in my wife's field either. The wages that were offered were so low that we decided it was better to move. It looked like we were going to lose our house and the housing market was still in rapid decline.

It would seem that the available work for the both of us had dried up. We were learning the lesson that there was actually no security in having a job alone to depend on for income. The realization that we were only a few months from bankruptcy after losing our jobs was becoming a reality.

At the time, I didn't have the real estate knowledge that I do now. This event is one of the reasons I ended up going into real estate.

Things looked grim. I was beginning to exhaust all my savings and unemployment was going to run out soon. We had just spent a large portion of our savings buying and fixing the house. It seemed we were on the verge of destitution, but this didn't stop us from taking action. After reviewing everything, we decided that we would move from the city back to the country.

Wages for the available jobs there were nearly the same. Best of all, the cost of living was much lower. We both had to make sacrifices to do this. My wife would be further from the art scene, and I would be in an area where there would be few management jobs available, especially those for my skill set and experience level. We would have to come up with a new game plan for our lives.

I made the decision to take whatever work I could find and simultaneously help my wife build her business. My wife is younger than I am; to me, this seemed like the most logical course. My career as a manager seemed to be over but I still wanted to go back to owning a business. Regardless, we had to decide what to do first, which was to get my wife's business and career off the ground.

We moved from a nice 3-bedroom home in an upscale neighborhood to a trailer that could barely fit our basic belongings. There was no air conditioning or various other luxuries we had previously enjoyed. We left much of what we had behind and stored the rest of our things in an old barn on the property.

Over the next 9 months, I worked as a cab driver and she took a job in a seamstress shop. We started getting some money set aside. We never fought about any of it. What would be the point? It wouldn't change anything. We knew the only thing we could do was stick to a plan and try to get back on our feet. As a cab driver, I was working 12 hours a day, 6 days a week. She was working for less than minimum wage.

I was pursuing a chance to become a private insurance adjuster on the side, studying at work during downtime in the car, while going to meetings any chance I could. One of these meetings was with an old associate. She was a real estate agent that had helped me buy a house about 20 years earlier using an owner-financing type of deal. I wanted to find another deal like this since my credit was now shot.

We couldn't go on living in the trailer anymore. I came to find out the agent had a place that had been wrecked by a previous tenant, and the owners lived overseas. My wife and I had the skills to fix the house, and after some discussion, we struck a deal. We decided we would offer services and home repairs in exchange for lower rent. Best of all, we would also receive the opportunity to buy the house later.

In the meantime, the cab company went out of business. I eventually found a new job as an overnight baker and we got to work on the new house. A month later, the house was livable again and we moved out of the trailer. It was a step in the right direction, a step up from the trailer to be sure. We once again had a house to live in.

Now my wife had space for her studio and we had a decent house to live in. Over the next five years, we constantly planned and moved towards our goals. She took a job with an area arts counsel. Thankfully, I also moved up to a much better paying job working as a chauffeur for a limo company.

During this entire time, we had been putting our heads together. She had been consistently taking work and building her business. Of course, this brought in more money too. Her first big break would later come when she landed a job for a major corporation, which would lead to her company finally getting off the ground.

The low paying small jobs would go by the wayside as she continued to grow her business. In addition, she applied to be part of a scenic artist union in the movie industry. It would take two attempts over the course of a year and a half, but she finally got in. The entire time, we were working together, helping one another reach our goals.

We continued to work together. I found a government job that paid more than the limousine company. By this time, I was aware of the mastermind principle and had been deeply studying real estate and the philosophies of success. Another year would go by as we built the groundwork and stabilized our finances.

Soon, we would be masterminding my move from the government job to becoming a real estate investor, a move which would lead me to being a life coach. When the time was right, and we were both in agreement, I would leave the government job.

Alas, a hitch. As we were planning this career change, the owners of the house we lived in decided to sell it. The real estate agent came up with a price that far exceeded anything we were willing to pay. Unfortunately, the move from the government job to real estate would have to wait. We again sat down and worked together to form a plan of action. The more we understood and saw the mastermind principle working for us, the more we used it.

Today we have weekly sit downs to go over every aspect of the week's events and form more plans to reach our goals. We look forward to this time together. We are not discussing problems and lamenting over them, rather, we are solving them to keep moving towards our goals.

We put our heads together and decided we would use my new real estate knowledge to find a house to buy rather than rent. After a month of steady searching, we found one. I struck a deal that would, in the end, net us well over $100,000 in equity in a new home we actually owned using an owner finance style deal.

We used cooperation at first and developed it into the stronger mastermind principle. We never argued about things. We worked in harmony and still do, always finding the positive side of each event. There was no animosity or selfishness, as we both had the same goals for each other.

In many cases, we spent several hours talking about our plans and going over ideas. We developed a plan to help her achieve some of her goals first. Then, when those goals were achieved, we developed a plan to move me along. We leapt our way to a more successful life and we are still doing this today.

I used my coaching skills, business knowledge and management experience to teach her everything I could about her business and how to improve her career. At the same time, I used my skills to start a small handyman business for extra income and increase my own knowledge about real estate.

Soon, I left the government job and became a full-time coach and real estate investor. Her career continued to blossom, and the money started to flow in. There were moments where we were down, but we always brought each other back up when it was needed. The selfless efforts from both of us, both using our minds to achieve one goal, had paid off. Today we have much bigger plans. Why not? It worked so well previously, why stop now?

The idea that you can do it yourself is false, as you can only go so far on your own. I have tried it several times and found the struggle extremely difficult. Without the support of a mastermind and the serious counsel derived from experience of others, I struggled endlessly. While you may be able to do it yourself to some extent, having a mastermind and strong counsel definitely speeds up the process.

Until I found my mastermind with my wife and then the ones with my businesses associates, succeeding was difficult. While we lived well and seemed to be able to overcome nearly every obstacle, there was still something missing when trying to push on to higher levels. We had goals, but they were too small. We had plans, but they were too shortsighted. Once we decided to go big and focus on greater goals, we started to see new levels of success. Dreams had become plans and those plans were put into action. The mastermind principle allowed us to pull from others and give back in return. We were reaching higher goals at a much faster pace.

Mastering the powers of your mind involves getting the help you need from others. Until you have support and cooperation from others, your journey will be far more difficult. The power of the team far exceeds the power of the individual. If you use a team and find a person to mastermind with, you will find success faster.

When the minds of loyal associates are put together, the power of combined thought is immense. If you want to reach true success, your associates should be of the same mindset. Once you apply the mindset and start to practice the philosophies, you will find each other.

Finding people becomes easier the more you practice and master the philosophies. Like minds attract one another. I went from having almost no friends and associates to having truly quality associates and friends. This all happened in a very short period of time. While it was slow at first, the pace increased steadily once things started moving.

The value of the mastermind cannot be overstated. When you put a mastermind together, you will know it. You will see the power of two or more minds working toward the same goals. The increase in thought and the value of those thoughts can propel you to success.

The Keys to Having a Successful Mastermind

- **Ability to work selflessly for each other and put the goal of the mastermind ahead of one's own interest.**

- **Never bringing negativity to the group or creating any kind of animosity. Animosity, selfishness, and discontent all bring the power of a mastermind down.**

The Mastermind should be working towards one goal. That goal is usually set by the founder and can be shared amongst the others. For instance, I have a two-person mastermind where we both use our different talents to help the other achieve their goals for real estate investing.

The mastermind my wife and I share allows us to work for each other, and work towards the same goals. By working together, we have both found more success in our lives; we have improved our lives greatly. We have done deals both together and separately. By invoking the mastermind principle, we also prevent partnership disagreements.

There is another mastermind which I was invited into, one based solely on the sharing of philosophies and learning more from each other about coaching and training. We all strengthen each other and help each other continue forward. By discussing what's happening in our lives and sharing our experiences, we are able to move forward with our own goals and create confirmations of the philosophies.

Putting a mastermind alliance together isn't always easy. In many cases, I have found that simple cooperation is a good form of working together and make things easier.

However, the benefits from working with people through other methods, including mere cooperation, are more limited compared to the mastermind.

By keeping a positive mindset and knowing you will find the right people, they tend to show up when you least expect it. If you're actively seeking a mastermind, you will find it.

The more people of quality you are around, the more people of quality you will find who can share in a mastermind with you or you in theirs. When you start seeking a mastermind and put your desires to work, you will find the people who understand the concept and know how to apply it.

I like to keep my true masterminds small. Others like to put together massive groups of people working for one goal. If you are ever invited to a mastermind, make sure you attend and remember the rules. Whatever is on the table, the group's goal is to benefit *that* person's goal. Leave your ego at home, bring your ideas and try to help the group reach the goals at hand.

The power of any size of mastermind cannot be overstated. The ability to truly merge two or more thought processes for the betterment of a single goal is a powerful means of finding success. Should the people in your group have all mastered certain aspects of the philosophies and the laws of nature, it works.

The very first mastermind, outside of the one with my wife, was based on the betterment of both people in the philosophies of success. This is a great way to start developing your skills. We support each other, point out each other's failings, and do so only for the benefit of the other.

This little group of two has changed the lives of not only ours, but of all those around us. We used this group to develop masteries of the philosophies, find our strengths and get input on our current plans.

There can be no value put on what all parties gain by this relationship. You become friends, business partners, and most importantly, have a mastermind support group. No matter how successful you become, having this type of support is priceless. I have yet to see anyone experiencing major success without having some form of mastermind cooperation in their lives.

All parties have only one goal: To help each other solve the problems they face or expand on the ideas they have. There is no better feeling than being a part of a group that helped someone else achieve a goal. Nor is there a better feeling than to have the support of those in the group, especially when you're facing your own challenges.

Taking Actions

WHAT IT MEANS TO TAKE ACTION

None of this philosophy works without taking action. You can have all the desire, passion, persistence, faith, trust, self-confidence, and perfection you need, but until you snap the reigns down on yourself and apply actions to set yourself in motion, nothing will happen.

Any action is better than no action, but quality actions bring quality results. When you feel there is nothing to do, you are probably overlooking something. There is always something you can do towards reaching your goals and bettering your life. Actions must take place in the world of interactions with others; studying alone in a room isn't taking enough action. While educating yourself is helpful, it is only a minor action. Education lays the foundation to take real actions towards your goal. While education and gaining knowledge is definitely an action, it's a small one. It's a necessity towards just getting started.

Taking action requires you to move forward in the material world. Living in isolation will not allow the universe to deliver opportunity. All minor actions add up; as you complete each of them, you better yourself and create more opportunities in your life. This happens when you reach outside your own universe and interact with other people in theirs.

You will hear many successful people tell stories of taking action when the opportunity arose. The first action to reach your goals after your education (or during) is to make new associations.

Get out there -- join groups, clubs, and meetings. Go to seminars, classes, and other events where you will be meeting like-minded people with similar goals. In fact, this is so important; I don't believe you can experience true success without taking this type of action.

Many people suffer from a fear of associating with others who have the same goals, thinking they are in some kind of competition with others with the same interests. While this may be true to some extent, it shouldn't stop you from getting out there and learning more about what it is you want to do. Meeting successful individuals in your field of interest can also help boost your knowledge of what it is you are trying to achieve. In addition, you will be meeting people who can help you, maybe even join you in a mastermind, or who can invite you to theirs.

If you want to become an actor, you don't hang out with mechanics. The reverse is true also. Changing who we associate with is an important first action to take. Each group has its own language also, and this is where your time spent educating yourself becomes important. You are increasing your specific IQ when you can fluently speak about your interests in an informed manner. It becomes easier to associate with people in that group because you speak their language.

If you have ever listened to people of specific careers talk with each other, you may feel like they are sometimes speaking a foreign language. A great example is listening to two doctors talking to one another. They use terms and phrases that you likely have never heard before, and surely, unless you're a doctor, won't understand. When you go out into the world and want to associate with others, you should at least be literate in their language.

This book is an important look into the language of success. While those you are speaking to may not understand Your Three Horses (unless they too have read the book) they will understand at least some of the concepts of success. You will recognize those who do and be able to discuss these philosophies with them.

The first real action I took after doing a lot of self-studying to becoming a real estate investor was to seek a mentor and coach. I wanted to meet someone who spoke both real estate language, as well as the familiar phrases of a Napoleon Hill, or similar, philosophy of success.

By taking the action to find new associates, I put myself on a path. I didn't realize how beneficial it was going to be at the time, or that it wouldn't be easy to find the person I was looking for. I visited 10 or 12 groups; some as far as two hours away. I listened to the speakers until I found the man who would become my mentor and coach, and eventually, close friend.

By this point, I didn't care what the cost would be or what it would take. My mentor taught at a real estate school he owned and offered paid private coaching. He spoke both the language of real estate and the language of success.

Most impressively, he subtly brought up topics about the philosophy of success. He spoke on many topics involving the proper mindset and taking actions. He spoke of finding pennies and giving thanks for each one you find. He also expressed the importance of being grateful for finding the penny, and how you would attract more money in doing so.

I immediately took action and approached him after the seminar, inquiring about hiring him to help me do deals. He told me that he offered private coaching. Two days later, we worked out a deal for the real estate school and coaching even though I didn't have the extra money. Like the philosophies teach, the money would come, and it did.

After my mentor recommended it to me, I bought a book called *The Secrets of the Millionaire Mind* by T. Harv Ecker. While reading this book, the philosophies within its pages became clear; I knew I had found my mentor and coach. He had also recommended other books, some of which I read twice over the next month. When he later asked if I read them, a conversation about those books and philosophies ensued.

Just like the teachings had taught me, what seemed (at the time) like a massive amount of money would come from my efforts. Accordingly, it was no problem paying for the coaching. I had convinced my own mind that the money for the coaching would come, and it came almost as quick as the payments came due.

He reaffirmed my actions by delivering exactly what I needed. I went the extra mile each week to drive two hours each way to his classes. I showed him I was serious and kept my word to him. When he first met me, I told him I had a lot of general and specific knowledge but needed guidance in applying it. He did a great job in helping me get everything I had learned from books and apply it to my goals.

I continued to take actions and do everything that he asked me to. I made an internal dedication and commitment to follow his lead. I was one of his first students to write one of the more complex style deals in real estate. Ever since he started walking me down the path of success, I have been finding success.

He didn't directly do anything for me. That's not what teachers do. They tell you how to find the path but it's up to you to make the journey.

By taking all the actions he wanted me to take, as well as some of my own, I expanded myself and my career in coaching. It seemed to take no time and the more actions I took, the more results I had. I can no longer make his classes regularly because I'm busy building my own business, real estate portfolio and expanding my goals. I still do, however, what I can and help him when he needs it. If he asks, I will be there for him.

Like anything in this philosophy, taking swift action while avoiding procrastination is essential. Procrastination is one of the main causes of failure. When we procrastinate, we don't take action. If we don't take action, we can't move forward.

The habit of procrastinating, as opposed to the habit of doing, can stop you entirely from ever making headway towards your goals. Taking positive, forward-moving actions will not happen if you are in the habit of procrastinating on the things that you need to be doing. Don't put off 'til tomorrow what you should have done yesterday -- just do it today.

Until you have a successful mindset, procrastination will set in. Once you are aware of the devastating effects of procrastination, you will start to catch yourself doing it. You will also begin to see others that tend to procrastinate and realize that this makes them unreliable, especially if you're trying to meet a deadline.

Most everything we do, either right or wrong, are actually habits we need to regain control of. The way we think and feel about a situation is as much habitual as it is simply emotional or rational. Almost everyone has some bad mental habits they need to address. You are not unique if you have them.

It's hard work to change the way you think and eliminate bad habits. Once you start to gain control of your habits, you can take positive action to change them. Simply being aware of your own bad habits and then taking action to change those habits will allow you to be in far more control of your life.

WE NEED TO TAKE ACTIONS TO:

- **Change our mindset on all levels**
- **View the world and its events in a positive light**
- **Finish what needs to be done now**
- **Find ways to expand our universe**
- **Take control of our reality**
- **Move forward towards our goals**
- **Change bad habits to good habits**
- **Change negative feelings into positive ones**
- **Develop a plan of action**
- **Take action on that plan**

Everything you try to achieve will require you to take some form of action, even developing the mental image of your goals. As discussed, you need to write down your major purpose. You will need to recite it, memorize it, and keep it in your mind as an obsession.

Of course, this takes both action and effort. However, doing this will build your passion for your purpose and allow you to continue to develop plans and spot opportunities.

You need to build your goals from the ground up, taking the mental and physical actions to put your desires and passions to work for you. Then, develop the mindset that causes you to endure and learn from hardships and setbacks. In doing so, you will strengthen your persistence and perseverance.

You also need to make hard decisions about with whom you surround yourself. Most importantly, you need to learn how to handle the negative people and/or naysayers currently in your life.

To be successful, or even happy, you will have to take continual actions to achieve each goal you set. There is no easy path or magic wand. You first need to take proper actions by controlling your own mind and developing good habits which lead to success. Then, put your actions out into the real world and continue to take every necessary action to grow.

The Three Horses are a metaphor to help you wrap your mind around what you need to do; they are the base to envision your goals in an organized manner. Their mental imagery is a way of organizing thoughts and applying them in the form of taking the actions necessary to reach your goals. They represent the powers of your mind. They will help to put your mind's powers to work for you instead of against you.

Once you have the concept of taking action down, move forward with confidence -- nothing can stop you. These philosophies work and have been proven. Many have come before me, attempting to both implement them and then to teach them. Those who put these concepts to work will succeed. Those who believe it is silly, or won't work, will get exactly what they think they will: failure.

Take action to conquer your fears and abolish your excuses. Take action to be responsible for what is happening in your own life. Do the work of self-evaluation and meditation on who you are and why you are in the position you are today. There is no fault; this isn't about blaming yourself or anyone else. It's about learning how to overcome your own beliefs and build new ones. It's about not allowing any setback or obstacles stop you.

If you haven't already started to overcome your weaknesses, you are procrastinating -- so knock it off and start taking action. Write down your major purpose or goals, do a meditation, and find out what it is that you truly want. Take action right now, don't wait. Unless you take action now, there will be no change in your future. You can read all the books you want and study all the philosophies you want, but until you take action you will get no results. The moment you decide to take action is the moment your life will start to change.

Read this book more than once if you need to (as a matter of fact I recommend it). Until you read it multiple times you will not see all that is offered within its pages. Read the other books recommended in my closing statements. Do the work and create your own future; start right now and don't procrastinate. If you have already started, then do more.

It took a long period of effort and hard work to get to where I am today. I went from a very poor English student to a published author. I went from poor to rich in less than 10 years. None of this would have ever happened had I not taken actions on my goals.

During the six weeks it took to write the first draft of this book, I was not just writing. I traded stock options for a nearly 50% profit, bought a property, and started bidding on a major purchase of a vacation real estate investment. After that, during edits, rewrites, multiple hitches and setbacks, I juggled yet other interests.

Regardless, I was going to finish this book in less than twelve weeks. That was the plan. I wanted it written, edited, and ready for publishing by a certain date. I didn't allow my other interests to be neglected to the point of stagnation, but I did make this book my first priority. I had to manage my time to keep both wheels on my chariot turning.

I realized that I had more than one goal and that it would take time and effort if I were going to achieve all of them at the same time. When focused on a project, I stayed with it until I was either worn out or simply needed some rest. When my brain was drained, and I couldn't write anymore, I shifted gears and went to look at properties.

When I wasn't looking at properties, I was trying to find ways to buy them. Every morning when I woke up, I wrote until a specific time and then researched my stock moves. When I needed a mental break from writing, I went to the stocks to see how they were doing. I didn't allow for any lost time during this process. I didn't have time to lose. *Do you have time to waste? Are your goals so unimportant you don't have time for them?* I have taken continual actions for months to reach my goals and timelines. You can do the same thing with whatever your interests are.

When I go to bed at night, I meditate on the day. I review what I did and didn't do, make plans for tomorrow and request inspiration for my interests each night. You can do this also; request inspiration daily and focus on your goals.

I kept my commitments to my wife, coaching students, tenants and business partners. I kept my commitments to my own coach and mentor. I take actions to achieve what it is I want to achieve. *Do you?*

Was the book done on time? No, but I didn't stop even through setbacks. I kept moving forward, never discouraged, falling back on my persistence, knowing that I would finish the book. I didn't leave myself any excuses for stopping and failing. I had the goal, the desire and the passion, and kept pushing forward. This is taking action and relying on your faith and trust to deliver.

If you are having problems getting started, try the Three Actions a Day Plan that we discussed earlier. Each morning when you wake up, write down three things you will achieve that day towards your goals, both long-term and immediate ones. Then make them happen. Fill your day with positive actions. I promise you will feel so good you won't want to stop. If you have some more time, add to the list. They needn't be huge goals, just get at least three things done daily.

When you start to do this, you are going to find small wins starting to pile up. You will be able to solve the setbacks that will come. You will feel good and find that by taking these actions daily you will reduce worry, anxiety and fear. Your goals will be closer to fruition with each passing day. Most importantly, by not procrastinating and taking actions you will feel good about each day's achievements. By the end of the day, you will feel empowered and invigorated, ready for the next day's challenges.

With each day that goes by, you will become better at managing your time, your life, and reaching your goals and dreams. Don't *think* you will have the things that you still want, *know* you already have them. Take the actions and time to develop the affirmations in your mind that you already have these things.

I have ridden my chariot through high fields and fast running rivers, all while barely seeing the obstacles. The metaphor of the chariot, horses and rider act as a guide to stay focused and organize your actions.

So, keep moving and take the actions needed. I want nothing more for the people who read this book to exceed my success. I want you to challenge yourself, be better than me. Heck, be better than everyone who's better than I am at this. Besides, I'm no one special. I have the same frailties and weaknesses that you do. Thinking differently about them sets me apart, and it is what will set you apart.

Take what's in these pages, all the experiences and knowledge I've shared from both others and myself. Find whatever resonates most and apply those lessons to your life. Take the lessons taught by those who came before you and use them for your own betterment. Simply knowing the philosophies will do nothing if you don't take actions to implement them into your own life.

The imagery of the horses is a tool to help you find out what actions you need to be taking in your life. If the horses don't resonate with you, then simply follow the plans and guidance in improving your life, most especially the way you think about your life.

Find your desires and create your purpose. Write it down with the price you will pay and a realistic time frame in which you expect to receive it.

Harness your passions so that you are enjoying what it is you are trying to achieve. This fuels your desires and gives you strength.

Use your fortitude and determination to have the perseverance to overcome the obstacles that will present themselves.

Have faith and trust in yourself and your purpose. Know that you are capable of reaching your goals and finding both success and happiness.

Work to improve yourself by improving how you think and see the world.

Become a better person, one that others will see as valuable. In this way we attract to us people of the highest quality.

Know that you are capable of achieving new goals and reaching new heights in life.

No matter what it is you want to be, take the actions needed to start a path towards that goal. If you want to be an actor, then take some acting classes or watch videos on acting methods while joining groups that focus on acting. No matter what it is you want to be, from a garage mechanic to a banker, you will never be one unless you start now.

Don't be a dreamer, be a doer. Turn your dream into a goal by having a plan. Have the heart, fortitude, and courage to make the change now. Build your chariot and power your horses, as there is no better time to start than now.

If you're reading this, it's likely you need to make a change. *So, what's stopping you?* The only thing that could be stopping you is *you*.

Don't wait! After all, waiting got you exactly where you're at right now. Remember, the universe came into existence when you opened your eyes. Harness the power within you, and go out there and start doing.

Do more than what needs to be done and you will be successful.

Closing Thoughts & Further Reading

When you live your dreams, you will inspire others to reach theirs.

Closing Thoughts:

It is with my sincerest gratitude that I thank you for having taken the time to read about my Three Horse Philosophy. I hope you found inspiration in these pages. I can only hope to hear from you one day to tell me about your success.

Maybe you will attend a lecture, or seek me out for direct help. Whatever the case may be, I want you to be successful and reach your dreams. Write me a letter or an email. Tell me your story.

The goal of this book was to fulfill one life's dream of becoming an author and teacher. Simply by reading this book, you have helped another person in fulfilling his life's dream. Take the words here and use them to improve your life. I hope this book will help you to reach your dreams.

Further Reading:

Upon completion of this book, it is highly recommended that you read the following books. When it comes to being successful and understanding the laws of nature, there is no better roadmap.

I tell you this because it was a book similar to this one that inspired me to return to the studies of these philosophies and start bettering my own life. In the application of these philosophies, I found that success was far easier to achieve than I ever allowed it to be.

Wattles, Wallace D., *The Science of Getting Rich,* Elizabeth Towne Publishing New York, 1910

Carnegie, Dale, *How to Stop Worrying and Start Living*, Kingswood, Surrey: Worlds Work, 1948.

Carnegie, Dale, *How to Win Friends and Influence People*, London: Vermilion, 1981.

Hill, Napoleon, *Think and Grow Rich,* Highlands Road Media, Inc. Los Angeles CA, 90046, 2004.

Kohe, J. Martin, *Your Greatest Power*, Kuala Lumpur: Napoleon Hill Associates, 2006.

Kohe, J. Martin, *The Secret of Doing Favors for People*, Kuala Lumpur: Napoleon Hill Associates, 2006.

Please visit my website: http://www.toddradus.com.

Made in the USA
San Bernardino, CA
15 February 2019